A Birth, a Death and a Barrelage

A History of

"The Hawthorn Farm"

In the area of Quinton-Oldbury

By Kate Creed

**Produced by Maxam Publishing
2008**

**Foreword by
Dr Michael Hall**

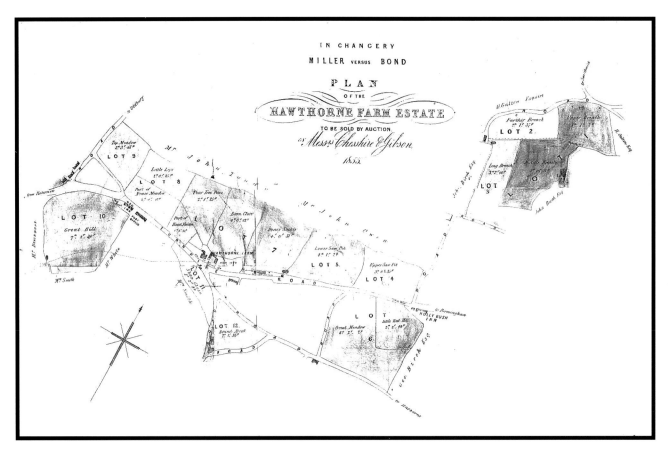

Figure 1 The Plan of Hawthorn Farm.

Front cover
Painting in oil of The Hawthorn Farm by W Nicholls.
Map taken from Bartholomew's Pocket Atlas and Guide to Birmingham.

ISBN 978-0-9560089-7-8.

First Published 2008 Maxam Publishing, West Midlands.

Book cover design by Harriet Creed 2008.

Printed and bound by Adlard Print & Reprographics Ltd,
Ruddington, Nottingham NG11 6HH.

In Chancery.

MILLER *v.* BOND.

NEAR BIRMINGHAM.

Particulars and Conditions of Sale

OF A

Very valuable and rapidly improving

FREEHOLD ESTATE,

Containing upwards of Sixty Acres of Land,

CALLED

THE HAWTHORN FARM,

Situate on the Hagley Turnpike Road, about Four
Miles from

BIRMINGHAM,

WHICH WILL BE SOLD BY AUCTION, BY

Messrs. CHESSHIRE & GIBSON,

AT THE

HEN AND CHICKENS HOTEL,

NEW STREET, BIRMINGHAM,

ON

THURSDAY, the 12th day of JULY, 1855,

At Four o'clock in the Afternoon,

IN TWELVE LOTS.

Figure 2 The sale details 1855.

Contents

Introduction
Ye Olde Rugacre

For like-minded individuals who enjoy looking at our local history, the people of Quinton, Oldbury and Warley are all very fortunate indeed to have had such a plethora of material enhancing our perception of an age gone by. Works by: Tom Bunting, Tony Rosser, Mike Hall and Andrew Maxam feed our thirst for local knowledge. However, this publication is quite unlike any of the previous works as it concentrates on the area now lost to us, known as "The Hawthorn Farm" at The Hawthorns.

This farm was one of the first to disappear from the local area, as it was sold in 1855 after being unused as a farm for several years. The passing of time and lost documents has hindered research, however, now the name of both The Hawthorn Farm and the hamlet known as The Hawthorns is brought to life in this book. It is no longer relegated to the title of a croft but is recaptured in name at least to be recognised as a place in the local community.

Research of the area around the farm has been a challenge due to the ever-changing boundaries and ecclesiastical shifts. The farmland is now divided by the main Hagley Road West in the borough of Oldbury in Sandwell on one side and Quinton Birmingham on the other. 'The Hawthorn Farm' was once in Worcestershire until The Quinton Parish Council took the decision to include The Quinton, (as it was then called) into Birmingham rather than Worcestershire. This decision was based on the fact that Quinton was so far out from the centre of Worcestershire it would be quite a while before it would obtain street lighting and have sewerage installed. As Quinton is only five miles from the town hall in Birmingham, it was considered closer and more accessible for a speedier resolution to the problem. To complicate it further Quinton was in the ecclesiastical district of Halesowen for civil reasons, Oldbury was divided into Warley Salop and Warley Wigorn of which Ridgacre was part. The Hawthorns was a tiny hamlet inside Quinton, closely adjoined to Ridgacre. So you can begin to see how many areas need to be researched in order to discover this history. Even this one time close-knit community would have had many developing addresses within it. An additional complication arose as the papers regarding the Troughtons and The Lytteltons are not all kept in one place and are scattered between, Birmingham, Coventry, Worcestershire, Shropshire and Staffordshire and some entries are missing entirely.

This busy urban land was once part of the larger greener grange of Halesowen manor, which in time became part of the Lyttelton estate. The tiny village of Rugacre, Quinton nestling onto the hills, was one of most charmingly situated rural villages of Worcestershire, sheltering tiny hamlets within it, including 'The Hawthorns'. In splendid isolation the hamlet of 'The Hawthorns' has been in the possession of Kings, a Colonel, a Chest maker and an outlandish philanderer.

From a wider perspective the delightfully picturesque Leasowes, which once offered tranquillity to the likes of the poets Shenstone and Thompson fringed The Hawthorns. Eminent Methodist pioneers, including John Wesley and Hugh Bourne have visited it and Howley Grange in The Quinton is listed as one of the hiding places of King Charles II. He escaped from the battle of Worcester in 1651 dressed as a farmer and furnished with some knowledge of this area as he was friends of the Littleton's (a precursor of the Lyttelton's). The battle of Worcester in 1651 was an attempt by the eldest son of Charles I to reclaim the throne and to re-establish the rule of the Crown in England.

The military chapter may seem a rather bizarre entry into a book based around this farm, however, the information uncovered is a fascinating glimpse into a world which is so far removed from daily life yet connected by the very fact that the main protagonist in this chapter owned The Hawthorn Farm through his marriage to Ann Troughton. It would have been a tragic mistake to omit such a career, which brings the worlds of Quinton and the Peninsular War closer than ever imagined possible.

Therefore, although it is a book based on local history I make no apology for its inclusion. You will find no fictitious characters or places here, but some key figures and many landmarks, some more interesting than others.

The research for this book evolved out of a growing interest rather than a predetermined plan to be published. It arrived at a point where it would have been egocentric not to share it. I hope you agree and that you find it as interesting to read as I had pleasure in writing it.

Kate Creed

Figure 2a The Holly Bush Shops Quinton.

Foreword

Dr Michael Hall

It is a great pleasure to respond to the author's invitation to write the foreword to this fascinating and unique voyage through a piece of Quinton's history. Big events have long been chronicled but most of us live on a small map rather than a large one and popular local history is a much more recent arrival on the scene.

I first heard of The Hawthorns over fifty years ago when my father talked of how his father had opened the Hawthorns Garage in Quinton in 1924 and sold petrol for 9d a gallon. The passing of "9d" and "gallon" into the pages of history underlines the importance of recording the past before it too disappears along with shillings, pence and imperial measurements.

Today The Hawthorns is sixty undistinguished acres of residential and commercial development on the western edge of a great metropolis. Kate Creed's painstaking research leads the reader through ten centuries to explore and explain its history. These sixty acres, strategically situated alongside the main highway from Birmingham to the greener lands of Worcestershire, encompass microcosm and spectrum: rural idyll set within the wider context of Shenstone's Leasowes and Lyttelton's Hagley; insights into the wealthy families who owned the land – Troughton, Hill, Nicholls, Galton – and the daily lives of the people who lived and worked here; the tragedies that traumatized them – attempted rape in 1843, murder in 1957. On the larger map Creed leads us to little Hawthorn's links with international events: the Peninsular War; mention in despatches; a monumental inscription in Jamaica. Local history is never merely micro; only scratch the surface and the macro appears.

Last, but by no means least, this is an attractively presented investigation, a happy marriage of text and picture, confirming the importance of contemporary illustration as historical source.

A Birth a Death and a Barrelage is an enigmatic but inviting title and local history owes a debt of gratitude to Kate Creed for sharing her labour of love with all who accept the invitation to travel with her through the history of The Hawthorns. It is a journey well worth taking and brings its own rewards.

Acknowledgements

I must give thanks to all the people that have helped and encouraged me in this rather longer than anticipated project. My list of thanks and appreciation is long however, it will inevitably leave someone out due to some error probably by my own hand, which is rather shameful but not intended. Please do not take offence, I have appreciated the input everyone has made and this book would not be complete without you.

I send thanks to my daughters, Natasha, whose spirit has encouraged me and to Harriet who as a little girl would sit quietly in libraries whilst mum looked at "old books and stuff", she has patiently awaited the completion of this long over due project and helped draw it to a conclusion by designing the cover.

To my friends, who have listened, advised and consoled me at times when I have been about to give up, you have made me laugh, loitered when you could have run and had the good grace and sense to know which action was appropriate at the time. You have sensed your presence would be of more value in a moment of gloom than any pill ever could be, I thank you for your spirit of enthusiasm and your patience for my interest in "all stuff that's old" and love you all, you know who you are.

To all of you that have allowed access to your deeds, photographs and family treasures, each one is appreciated, copied and returned. Your consistent enthusiasm for this project has kept me going at times when I have considered this perhaps just a little too ambitious a task for me to continue with.

To include:

Mr Mrs Atack.

Michael Alcock.

Tom Alcock.

John Bailey.

Janice and John Barnett.

The Bass Museum Burton- on Trent.

David Browning.

Lily Browning.

Mrs Winnie Bartleet.

Birmingham Reference Library.

Birmingham City Archives NRA 143

Irene and Peter Boot.

Helen Braznall and family.

Vera Carey and family.

Coventry Archives.

Cradley Library.

The Darwin family of Perry Hill particularly Emily.

The Diocesans Record Office, Birmingham.

Lucy Dearn.

Dudley Library Services.

Forster and Wheeler solicitors.

Toby Fountaine.

Mrs Valerie Glover/ Hacket.

Lynda Hall.

Emily Harold.

Jeff and Noelle Heath.

Mrs Hibbard.

Dorothy Hughes.

Pam and Roger Hickman.

Mr and Mrs Jeanerette.

Carol and Martin Lindop.

London and North family history society.

The Maidstone Museum and Art Gallery.

Mrs Moulding.

Mrs Mylchrist.

The National Army Museum.

Roy Parsons.

Mr and Mrs Parton.

The Partridge family of Trevanie Avenue.

Mr and Mrs Paxton.

The Post Office Heritage London.

The Powell family.

The Public Record Office.

Regimental Museum Record Office.

Betty Rose.

The Royal Cambrian Academy Conwy.

Nickie Sandford.

Sandwell Council (Sandwell roads history).

Sandwell Community History and Archives service. Ref BS/MB NRA 146.

Gladys Shaw.

Shropshire County Council.

Adrian and Carl Tighe for matters of a military nature.

Colonel. H B Waring OBE, The Queens Own West Kent Regiment.

Barbara Westall.

Horace Wilson

Mrs Wisdell.

Irene Hancox nee Witcomb.

Joyce Heath nee Witcomb.

Worcester Record Office.

Gladys Creed Nee Witcomb, deceased, my mother in law and great friend.

Dave Yates.

Gabrielle and Martin Hurst.

Ian and Karen Tighe.

My thanks to John Cattermole who has endured conversations about people and places unknown to him with good grace and patience.

To "my men" as my children used to say, originally meeting just to exchange pictures of old Quinton this evolved into a cluster group and became **Q**uinton **H**istory **S**ociety. As the thoughts of an ever-growing group proved too onerous a task for us, the group was formally created into the **Q**uinton **L**ocal **H**istory **S**ociety with Bernard Taylor at the helm. My thanks to Bernard for an ever-helpful interest in this project, to David Hassall, for his gentle calm approach and his very informed relatives, to Anthony Rosser for his encouragement and advice on how not to produce a book. Andrew Maxam a friend of now many years has who has allowed the use of some of his treasured photographs and Mike Hall for his wise words advice and kindness. Their interest, enthusiasm and tireless chats have been an inspiration.

To the many more people that have contributed in any way what so ever, I thank you for your support.

Figure 2b Where The Hawthorn Farm once stood.

Chapter One

The earliest record available of the land was made available to us by William the Conqueror, who invaded England in 1066 and commissioned Domesday Book in December 1085. The first draft was completed in August 1086 and contained records for 13,418 settlements in the English counties south of the rivers Ribble and Tees (the border with Scotland at the time). The local entry reads;

> *"In the clent hundred, Earl Roger holds of the King, a Manor called Halas, it contains ten hides, there are in demesne four caractes, and thirty six villens and eighteen borders, four rad men, a church with two priests, among them forty one ploughs and a half, there are eight bondmen and two bondswomen. of this land roger the huntsman holds of the earl one hide and a half, he has there, one carucate and six villens and four borders, with five ploughs, it is worth yearly 25s".*

The Manor changed hands frequently before the Abbey was founded including to name but a few, Earl Roger of Shrewsbury 1075-1094 and David ap Owen 1177-1204. In 1274 it is referred to as 'Ridgacre', with plenty of variations on the spelling; Rugacre, Ruggeacre all being interspersed with the name Quinton, but all effectively the same place. The name Ridgacre being retained by the lane and the road only and is rarely if ever used as an area address now. The older generation will fondly recall its usage, pronouncing it as "ridge a ker" which meant the "ploughed land on the ridge", but as population in the area increased in more recent years, Quinton and Ridgacre areas began to develop into their own separate areas.

In 1218 until its dissolution in 1539, Quinton was held under the jurisdiction of the Abbot and in 1272, he was authorised to grant the town of Halas, 'Borough status'. The decisions of the court would have affected the rural Quintonians, in many ways "Particularly those relating to agriculture. They were required to do six days of ploughing and six days of harrowing every lent for every thirty acres of land they held. They had to grind their own corn at the Abbots mill unless it was out of order" (Rosser 1998.141).

The last Abbot resigned in 1539 and the Manor of Hales, including Warley Salop and Warley Wigorn was granted to Sir John Dudley, a supporter of King Henry VIII, but ultimately the land was sold and or in part given to his brother when Sir John was executed and his cousins imprisoned. The lands of Halesowen were taken from the family temporarily but were restored to Robert Dudley and his wife Amy in 1555. Robert purchased his deceased brothers share in the land and went on to sell it to sitting tenants George Tuckey and business partner Thomas Blount, for £3,000 which included both Warley Salop and Warley Wigorn in 1558.

Rosser's book *The Quinton and Roundabout, Volume one,* delves a little more into the ancient past with records of court rolls and details of the Abbey and the monks, whose reputation varies from humble husbandry types to ruthless unrelenting landlords. There would be little point in repeating his text here but Rosser's work finishes his chapter on the demise of the Abbey with the unsympathetic words of William Shenstone; whose land abutted the Lyttelton's estate, both estates being once part of the Abbey,

> Here if my vista point the mouldering pile
> Where hood and cowl devotions aspects wore
> I trace the tottering relics with a smile
> To think the mental bondage is no more (1998.142).

Blount and Tuckey sold the land including a large proportion of 'The Hawthorn Farm' to the Lytteltons by way of a 1000-year lease. It is important to note that the farm was not sold in its entirety, the estate documents refer to 'The Hawthorn Farm' at different junctures in the estate's history. It is not clear exactly which parts were sold until 1855 and even then there was a dispute over unproven ownership, which will be revisited later with the dissolution of the farm.

The Lytteltons owned much of the land on the north east of Worcester and many of the older maps indicate the extent of their wealth. In 1562, Sir John Lyttelton became Lord of the Manor of Hagley at a time when the Lyttelton's were papists. This may have caused tensions with the protestant monarch and government as the church at Hagley Hall fell under their guiding hands. However, whatever tensions there were, they fell apart soon after the gunpowder plot and over the centuries a greater partnership has evolved (Deeley. 9).

The house that we know today as Hagley Hall was built between 1754 and 1760, prior to that there stood an old Jacobean building in which George Lyttelton nephew of Charles Lyttelton governor general of Jamaica was born. George and his parents Sir Thomas Lyttelton and Christina Temple were the last family to live in the old building before moving in to the new house, within the park at Hagley.

We owe the landscaping of Hagley Park to George, Lord Lyttelton (1709-1773) who was known as the 'good' Lord Lyttelton and was elevated to peerage in 1759 for his services to the crown. Although he entered parliament in 1730 he spent a great deal of time at his Hagley estate in spite of holding high political office. He enjoyed the same pursuits as his friend and neighbour William Shenstone (1714-1763), who lived nearby; Shenstone was one of the earliest practitioners of landscape gardening to develop his own ideas on his own estate. He was well known for his poetry and often linked it to local history themes. He mentions Hagley in Elegy XIII: *Works in Verse and Prose*, which refers to a more violent time where Anglo-Saxon regicide took place but "since Lyttelton has crown'd the sweet domain / With softer pleasures, and with fairer fame' it has become a more tranquil place" (Harrington.27). Shenstone also wrote *Dialogues of the dead* and regularly entertained the greatest poets and artists of the period at Hagley with Lyttelton including; Walpole, Pope, Gray, Addison, James Thomson and Richard Wilson who were frequent visitors to the park, sometimes writing elegies to record the splendour of the Hagley landscape, or painting family portraits.

Two examples of the appreciation of the park are Horace Walpole who although notoriously hard to please, wrote, "I wore out my eyes with gazing, my feet with climbing, and my tongue and vocabulary with commending" after his visit in 1753.

The second example comes from James Thomson;

An extract from James Thomson's 1774 edition: *The Seasons*
An extract from Spring, Hagley Park

These are the sacred feelings of thy heart (904)
Thy heart informed by reason's purer ray.
O Lyttelton the friend! Thy passions thus
And meditations vary, as at large,
Courting the muse, through Hagley park you stray
Thy British Tempe! There along the dale
With woods o'erhung, and shagged with mossy rocks
Whence on each hand the gushing waters play,
And down the rough cascade white-dashing waters fall
Or glean in lengthened vista through the trees (913)

Meantime you gain the height, from whose fair brow (950)
The bursting prospect spreads immense around:
And, snatched o'er hill and dale, and wood and lawn,
And verdant field, and darkened heath between,
And villages embosomed soft in trees,
And spiry towns by surging columns marked
Of household smoke, your eye excursive roams-
Wide stretching from the Hall in whose kind haunt
The hospitable Genuis lingers still (958).

There is much to be gleaned from this poetry; it confirms his friendship with Lyttelton and his association with the park, whilst at the same time demonstrates his appreciation of the vista. He talks of his leisurely walk through undulating hills and valleys of the park as he walks freely to stray where he will, no labouring here for the Lyttelton's or their guests. He emphasises the height of the high hills where waterfalls drop and the size of the lands in the lengthened vista. The second verse walks you along highs and the lows of the green lush to the villages whose chimneys have replaced the trees and whose smoke fills the air well beyond the hall. One of the villages he would have been able to see was Quinton, Rugacre.

The tranquillity enjoyed by the poets was disrupted, at least partially, as the estate, which once sprawled its way across Quinton and beyond was split and by some measure, sold off. "The Hawthorn Farm" was part of that sale and the lease of 1000 years was sold. Mr Samuel Troughton commenced negotiations on 22nd, May 1773. The indenture reads, "whereby the right honourable Thomas Lyttelton conveys to Samuel Troughton and Joseph Troughton, this 'maise farm' and premises in the parish of 'Halewoen' for the repayment of two thousand pounds"(MS.9273) and is signed on 20th September 1774 and witnessed by John Dudley and Robert Bloomer.

Various other farms were sold off over the coming years, including Bristnall fields, perhaps to accommodate the spiralling costs of building and furnishing their new house, which we know today, but possibly attributed to feeding a passion beyond architecture and fashionable décor. Thomas, who was nicknamed 'naughty Tom' had quite a reputation, he enjoyed the very best that he could take in life and died in 1779 at the tender age of 35 as a very *old* man, taking the peerage he acquired with him as although had married Aphia Peach he left no issue.

Thomas had many affairs but one in particular is prolifically recorded. Thomas began an affair with a Mrs Amphlett, her damaged marriage survived but it left her a disgraced woman that could not come to terms with her situation, and resultantly she committed suicide. Her daughter, Sarah aged sixteen was to replace young Thomas's affections, as did her younger sister Mary. His final descent into the moral pit of evil was to switch his affections to the younger third sister, Eliza, who was the result of the initial affair with Mrs Amphlett. Descriptions of his devilish deeds vary, newspaper cuttings at the time reveal that an anonymous pamphleteer circulated a damming indictment in which Lord Lyttelton was called "Lord Lucifer" and his mansion described as "Hell House". He reputedly laughed the condemnation and appeared impervious to such earthly criticism. Naughty Tom's punishment may have come from a higher plane as the story gathers pace and intrigue. He is said to have had a great dislike of being alone and a constitutional melancholy that drove him into society. He held an office under the Government in Ireland and on his return from it, suffered from suffocating fits, proceeding either from indigestion or from heart disease. Finding himself ill on the evening of Nov. 24th, he retired early to bed. His servant gave him the medicine ordered for these attacks and then left him.

Timbs in Valentine tells the tale,

"He had not been gone long when Lord Lyttelton, who believed himself to have been awake, heard a gentle fluttering of wings in his room; and while he listened to it with some surprise, he heard footsteps approaching the bed. Curious to know what caused these sounds, he sat up in bed, and was astonished to see a lovely female form all in white, with a small bird perched on her hand, standing by his bed. He was speechless from surprise, and she spoke to him. She bade him prepare himself, for that he would shortly die. Lyttelton inquired at once how long he had to live. The vision answered, "Not three days, and you will depart at the hour of twelve". When he arose in the morning, he felt so uneasy that he could not help telling his dream or vision at the breakfast-table to his assembled guests. But he tried to convince himself that it was only a common dream. He said he had had some trouble to catch a robin in the greenhouse at Pitt Place a few days before, meaning to set it free - that might account for the bird; but every one saw that he was uneasy and gloomy, and that his thoughts dwelt upon the subject. He grew more composed during the day; attended the House of Lords, and delivered two brilliant and witty speeches.

The second day passed much in the same manner. The third day at dinner, Lord Lyttelton rallied wonderfully, and exclaimed as the cloth was removed, "Richard's himself again". Admiral Wolseley and his other guests have stated that his spirits were high, and that his conversation was remarkable for wit and brilliancy. But, as the evening wore on, his mood changed to restlessness and despondency. To prevent his becoming the victim of mere imagination, they had all put on their watches half an hour, and had, with the connivance of his valet and steward, altered all the clocks and his own watch, putting them on half an hour, so that when Lord Lyttelton believed it to be half-past eleven, it was in reality only eleven o'clock. About this time he complained of feeling very tired, and retired to bed; when there he showed great uneasiness; looked often at his watch and consulted that of his valet. At a few minutes to twelve, he held both watches to his ear; was pleased to find they were going; and that it was a quarter-past twelve. "This mysterious lady is not a true prophetess, I find," he said; "give me my medicine. I will wait no longer." The valet went into the next room to get it, but thinking he heard his lord breathing unusually hard, he hurried back to the room He found Lord Lyttelton dying. He called for help, and Lord Fortescue, the Miss Amphlet's, cousins of the dying man, and their companion, Mrs Hood, hastened into the room; they were only in time to see him die - exactly at twelve o'clock.

At the very hour he expired a Mr Andrews, one of his most intimate friends, imagined that he saw Lord Lyttelton standing by his bedside, and thinking it was some joke on his part, reproached him for coming to Dartford Mills without notice, and jumped out of bed to ring and order a room to be prepared for his unexpected guest. But, when he looked round his strange visitor was gone. The servant answered the bell, and Mr Andrews asked if he had met Lord Lyttelton. Of course the answer was in the negative. Mr. Andrews, still suspecting a practical joke, dressed himself, and searched everywhere for his friend. He was still suspecting a hoax, when at four o'clock next day, an express arrived telling him that Lord Lyttelton was dead. We confess that this second ghost is much more puzzling than the first, which may have proceeded wholly from a melancholy imagination, feeling the approach of death. Yet the whole subject is full of mystery; and incredible to us nineteenth-century people; though for our own part we believe with Shakespeare that there are "more things in heaven and earth than are dreamt of in our philosophy" (Timbs).

This story varies slightly in detail from source to source, but the basic narrative remains the same. He lived to extremes in all that he undertook; he enjoyed life to the full and managed to be the topic of conversation in both life and death. The assets acquired from the sale of The Hawthorn Farm would have furnished his *spirited* life style for the very brief four-five remaining years of his life.

Once again "The Hawthorn Farm" experienced another change of ownership as it moved from a naughty Tom to an entrepreneurial Sam and his brother Joseph. The Troughtons originally came from Coventry and were related to Dr Nathaniel Troughton, one of the first artists to record the changing face of Coventry, whose sketches are frequently used and referred to locally throughout the city.

Samuel Troughton was an entrepreneur who owned not only the farm but also many businesses around the midlands. He is listed in Swinneys directory of 1775 as a plater and jappaner at 13 Edmund Street. The company made "tables, waiters' trays, baskets and tea chests of infinite and beautiful variety and of various prizes"(Swinneys). The farmland and plating businesses were just two facets in Troughton's busy life, he also had partnerships with his son and in more recent years with a gentleman by the name of Ward, the latter was dissolved by 1777. Troughton was also father to three daughters Ann, Susanagh and Elizabeth. When Elizabeth died, her will reveals that 'The Hawthorn Farm' was at that time 62 acres of arable farming land, this was whittled down over the coming decades but is unclear as to exactly what became of it until the last remaining pieces were sold in 1855.

Samuel Troughton died in 1782 leaving his businesses to his surviving children, Ann and Samuel junior. Samuel died prematurely in 1790 and he left his estate to Ann. As with many wills there are usually a few problems and this one was no exception. Troughton left most of his estate to Ann but the farm was only a part of the estate and in turn not all of it was hers to dispose of. The problem was not to manifest itself until Ann died many years later when the families concerned contested her will, this is evident on the farm's sale notice details, where Millar and Bond battle for their perceived rights.

Bristnall fields were sold off for £250 and parts of The Hawthorn Farm for an undisclosed sum in order to fulfill some of Troughton's wishes. His will also left some private belongings to William Sutton in the parish of Harborne, but as some of his properties were sold prior to his death this led to complication with his will. A letter dated 1810, from J Humphries refers to part of the problems as the house in Edmund Street, where his japanning business operated, was not his to dispose of.

"Supposing however the purchaser to be fully satisfied on these points then I conceive that the ecclesi-astical court granted probate of Samuel Troughtons unexecuted will, the leaseholds being part of his personal estate "trapped" by this with ought now to be sold under the trusts of it. The first trust being for payments of debt will exonerate the purchasers from seeing to be application of this money but still I think it prudent especially as this trust has so long remained unexecuted...Mrs Hill should be added to the trustees for sale under her late brothers will".

We have a glimpse of the problems that fell upon Ann to try and settle, however, she did not succeed and the battle problems led to the court case upon her death.

It was rather difficult to glean very much more information on the farm at this time other than what census and estate maps can provide. Newspapers fil! some gaps in local historical events but there is little information around for this period. A void in information from maps, papers and photographs therefore looked probable for this project. However, fortunately, there was an artist at work and he successfully fills that gap, a painting entitled, "The Hawthorn Farm", by W. Nicholls from a private family collection came to the surface.

The Hawthorn Farm

This idyllic scene painted in oils is the quiet country scene of this Worcestershire farm over one hundred and fifty years ago. It is a brief glimpse into Quinton life where the children are playing carefree and the cows amble along paces away from where the locals today visit the building society, collect a pizza, or hire a party costume. The farm buildings can be seen at a later time in history as they become homes to the cottage industries in figure 43. When the buildings were knocked down the new row of shops were built further back, enabling a straighter road into Birmingham, therefore this farm building would have been very close to what is now the main road.

Figure 3 Painting in oil of The Hawthorn Farm By W Nicholls.

Thomas Troughton's Era

The lease

26th May 1773 assignment of 1000 years term in trust for

Mr Samuel Troughton.

22nd 23rd December 1773 Indenture of lease and release whereby the right honourable

Thomas Lyttelton for the consideration in this release mentioned conveys to said Thomas

Troughton and his trustee Joseph Troughton a certain maize farm, lands and premises situate

and being in the parish of Halesowen in the county of Salop and Worcester or one of them.

I do acknowledge that have this day received of Mr Samuel Troughton the several deeds and

writings I the above abstract mentioned which I promise to keep as safe as my own and redeliv-

er up the same safe and un…. Upon repayment of two thousand pounds and the interest which

shall at that time become due and payable until such deeds and writings shall be destroyed by fire

or any other inevitable accident as witnessed my hand this 20th day of September 1774.

Witnessed hereto

R Bloomer

John Dudley

Figure 4 The lease agreement from Lyttelton Troughton.

The painting was hidden away until 1998 and is to date the only view available of the farmhouse. Previously there had only been map references and photographs of the cottage industries that survived the farms closure.

"The Hawthorn Farm" was one of the first farms to die locally due to its importance geographically in linking Birmingham and Worcester. Therefore, there are few people to have any recollections of there ever having been a farm here and even fewer can recall family connections to it. There are a few token gestures to the name "Hawthorn", we have Hawthorn Croft and Hawthorn flats but nothing else remains. We are fortunate indeed to have this material and it is a privilege to be able to share what little there is with the reader. A Nicholls family lived at The Hawthorn Farm in 1841 and appear on the census records as, Thomas Nicholls with his wife Elizabeth, Henry age 40 and his wife Rebecca age 20 with their baby daughter Ann. Then in 1851, Henry Nicholds had taken over the tenancy and lived with his five children, Ann, Rebecca, Henry and William aged seven, could this William have been the artist? Was the Nicholds a spelling error in the record? The connection is tenuous but possible. Whilst it seems unlikely that a working farmer's son would have had the resources to paint, it is not totally impossible as it was a large farm of over 60 acres and the family were able to employ servants and labourers.

W. Nicholls exhibited from 1875 to 1899, he exhibited 21 works at the Royal Society of Birmingham Artists between 1875 and 1899. If it was the same W. Nicholls then the seven year old budding artist would have been exhibiting in Birmingham from the age of 31 to 55 and painting prolifically as many of his works are listed in the exhibition catalogues. If it wasn't the same man then who ever he was he managed to capture both the scenic beauties all around the area and our attention!

The listed works are:

1863   (Autumn) Autumnal view from the top of Richmond Hill Surrey

1871   (Autumn) Cornfield Rotton Park

1871   Frankley Church Worcestershire

1872   Old cottages, not listed as Quinton but suggested to be so

1872   Lane Scene

1872   Autumn a Staffordshire cottage

1875   (Spring) Old Cottages Worcestershire.

1875   (Autumn) Lane Scene, Perry Barr (Watercolour)

1876   The Lane Scene Yardley

1876   Lane Scene Northfield

1881   Barston Pool Sutton Pool

1882   An evening at Bracebridge pool Sutton Park

1882   Aston Church Evening

1883   In summer time Worcestershire

1884   (Spring) Enville Corrol

1884   (Spring) The old Road over the Lickey Hills

1888   (Spring) The Old Watermill Portlock Somersetshire

Three cards in the index at R.S.B.A. are misplaced so there is no record of the remaining pictures at that source. Two of the paintings not exhibited but are known are Hawthorn Farm (date unknown) and Redhall farm (date unknown).

Mrs Jeaneret had several more paintings from W. Nicholls but knew very little about the artist. The paintings had been in Mrs Jeaneret's family on her father's side for many years and she had been intrigued as to their history. Apparently, her grandparents, Mr and Mrs Field, purchased the paintings whilst living at Meadow Road in Quinton, her Grandfather was a cabinetmaker there. Mr and Mrs Field later bought some of other works as a wedding gift for Mrs Jeaneret's parents and the pictures were framed in Bearwood.

The paintings are:

Sketch Cold bath pool near Moseley

Sketch, Worlds End near Harborne 1878

Bagots Park

Bagots Park near Abbots Bromley

Howley Grange. 1874

Foley's House Quinton. 1880

another is un-titled but thought possibly to be Perry Hill farm (With twisted brickwork)

Two more, which are unnamed

There is no reference to him as a professional artist and there is no record of him ever having exhibited in London. Therefore, a local, enthusiastic amateur would probably describe him best. I think we should now add to that "of note" as he had the foresight to paint the farm recording it for future generations and bringing it back for us, in what could have been a dose of nostalgia or a commission, however, the result is the same.

Two of the farms he painted have a connection other than having been painted by the same artist. John Wood was a tenant on land still referred to as The Hawthorns during the late 1880's. His daughter Emma married Thomas George Wyrley Birch, Thomas's father George had owned Redhall farm from the mid 1850's.This would suggest that these two farms were painted or perhaps commissioned because of the family connection or perhaps by this time owned by the same. It is unfortunate that the whereabouts of many of these paintings remain for now unknown.

The Wyrleys' were the earliest family recorded as being seated at Hamstead. They came from Little Wyrley and although some of them were referred to de Hamstede, they finally adopted the name de Wyrley. They continued to hold Hamstead for generations and became the largest landholders in Handsworth. The Wyrleys became connected to the Birches through marriage.

A sale at The Hawthorn Farm

This takes place in 1847, after the Nicholls family left. The goods are the property of Mr Benjamin Thomas and include all the farming implements one would expect, for instance the double plough goes to Mr Cleeton for one pound and three Heifers go for nine pounds and five shillings to Mr Bromley. It suggests that the farm had may have been selling off the farming implements from as early as 1847.The contents of the house and more agricultural equipment was auctioned in 1849 when they are recorded as the property of Mr Thomas Davies. These two sales indicate that either the farm down sized at this period prior to Mr Nicholds (Nicholls) taking residence or the land was simply used as an auction site due to its proximity to the road. By the time the farm was auctioned off in 1855, Mr Cooper was leasing the farmhouse, which was later used for cottage industries.

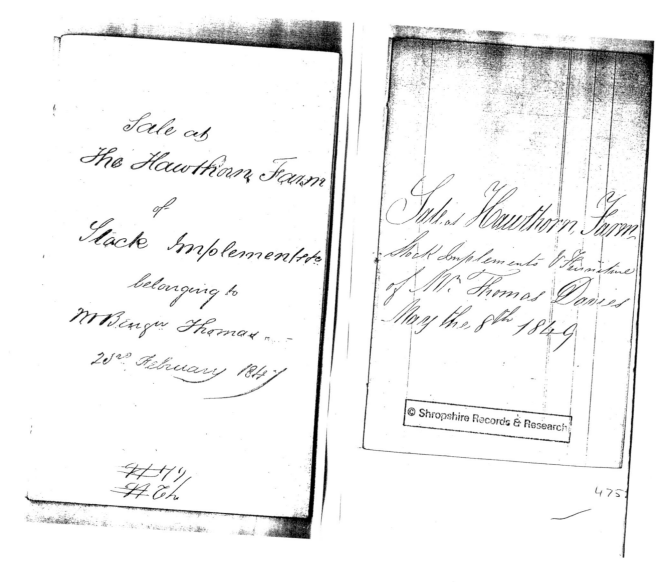

Figure 5 Sales of contents and farming implements on The Hawthorn Farm.

Chapter Two

To Matters Military

Figure 6 Advance on Vittoria.

Advance on Vittoria, Chris Collingwood.
The 13th Light Dragoons cross a small river as part of Wellington's armies advance on Vittoria in June 1813 during the Peninsula Campaign.

From Troughton to Hill

Ann Troughton outlived her sisters Susannah and Elizabeth by many years as they both died in early adulthood, each leaving their estates to Ann. Her brother, Samuel Bryan Troughton had inherited one of his father's japanning businesses in Birmingham and this too fell to Ann upon his death.

She was unmarried at the time of her father's death and as the last surviving daughter; she inherited most of his estate, therefore well provided for.

Marriage

"On 1st September 1797 at Polesworth Church

in Warwick, Ann Troughton only surviving daughter of the

late Samuel Troughton married Captain Charles Hill of the 50th Regiment of Foot".

Figure 7 The Gazette 1797.

The marriage to Charles took place in her hometown of Polesworth, near Tamworth Warwickshire and was witnessed by Mary Cottrell and Richard Aldridge, names that will appear much later. She spent little time there after her marriage and moved to London, presumably to be closer to her husband's military base or to be close to the wives of other military personnel. She enjoyed living at some prestigious addresses, one being Connaught Terrace near Connaught Square, which at the time was surrounded by parkland. Shops and offices have since replaced the Terrace, but the square remains. Even in the present day, it is a very charming place to live, with its attractive and well-maintained Edwardian frontages complete with white painted facades, spoiled only by the noise and pollution of the main Edgware Road.

Peter Thorold writes in *The London Rich* of it as "an area designed for the rich by the rich" (204) and it was one of the first such areas built in 1807. When she applied for an army pension from the King, she gave her address as a private address in Portland Place and a later address at Cavendish Place. Neither address was for the poor of London, evidence enough to suggest she did not suffer in Charles' absence. She probably had very little to do with the farm, other than arranging to have the rents collected from her tenants by an agent at The Red Lion public house, which stood on what is now the central reservation on the Hagley Road West.

As the wife of a soldier there seems very little to be able to say about Ann, other than she remained childless and was made a widow in 1819. However, her husband had a distinguished military career, which would be very remiss to omit, as it is a rarity to bring a military life, the Peninsular War, Wellington and a mention of Nelson so close to home. Whilst Hill spent the majority of his career with his regiment, The 50th Foot in either England or Cork in Ireland, not all of it was so routine.

A television series entitled "Sharpe", based on the books by Bernard Cornwall are supposedly tales of fictitious characters placed in real historic time. These events closely resemble some of the battles and skirmishes Hill experienced whilst in the Peninsular.

Both the book and the series Sharpe's Honour in particular, covers the battle of Vitoria*.

Were any of the incidents based on Hill's experiences or those of his regiment? Perhaps you may wish to read both and make the judgment for yourself.

The series, based on the books written by Bernard Cornwall are supposedly tales of fictitious characters placed in real historic time. Were any of the experiences based on Hill's experiences or those of his regiment? Perhaps you may want to read both and make the judgment for yourself.

* The spelling of campaigns, references and personnel vary, but remain as recorded; "Vittoria" as spelt in Fylers book, is "Vitoria" on Hill's tombstone and in Cornwall's books Sharpe's books. There are other inconsistencies but the reader will have to accept these nuances, as we did not fight these battles, nor pay the price, so we must live with the authorial variances in spelling, they will be marked with a star * where possible.

The highlights of his career are listed with his promotions, uniforms, colours, battles, and medals, ending with a final poignant farewell from Ann.

The history of the 50th title

Much of the information in this section comes from Colonel Fylers book, *The History of 50th or (The Queens own regiment)* from the earliest year to 1881 (which has long since been out of print) but has been an invaluable primary source. However, as Fyler was a member of the regiment, there are also other publications referred to for a more balanced perspective.

Colonel Fyler was made Lieutenant Colonel on the 4th July 1880; he researched and recorded its history during his career. Each regiment of the British army has its own history, traditions, and insignias and the 50th was no exception. The subject of regimental title has caused great consternation over the years and even now seems to arouse emotions, so it seems appropriate to included some of its history and title variances in order to understand a little of the regiment and how The Queens Own Regiment 50th (The Title) has frequently been challenged or changed.

"A difference of opinion has existed for some time, whether this title should be (Queens Own), or the Queens Own. It will be noticed that in a letter which is taken from the orderly room records, the words "or the" are included in the brackets but without capitals, this has led to the (Queens Own) being generally adopted." It is also adopted on the Indian monument in Canterbury Cathedral.

"On the other hand a letter from Lord Fitzroy Somerset on 1st February 1831 to Officer Commanding 50th Regiment, on the subject of this title, calls it "The Queens Own". A letter was then written to the Adjutant General Department and he replied – "the title of the 50th Regiment was changed on 14th January 1831 from the Duke of Clarences Regiment to the "50th or Queens Own" (2.).

The 50th, originally known as "The 7th Marines", disbanded in 1748, and reformed for The Seven-Year War, with a blur existing between military and naval involvement. We know of course that the 50th Regiment existed for far longer than that, as Charles Hill served in it up to 1819. The regiment was quartered at various stations in Ireland until the latter part of 1772, then embarking for Jamaica during the beginning of 1773. The regiment remained in Jamaica until the beginning of 1776 and ordered to North America where it was broken up, all men fit for duty were drafted to reinforce other regiments. The staff returned to Salisbury England to recruit up to their full strength in 1776, a task that took two years to complete.

Charles Hill joined as Ensign in 1778 and on 31st August 1782, the Corp assumed the title of "50th or West Kent Regiment". In 1831, as the Duke of Clarence came to the throne, the 50th Regiment was authorised to assume the title of 50th Queens Own instead of the Duke of Clarence's Regiment and facings changed from black to blue. Therefore, given what we now know to be a sensitive issue for the purpose of this book, it shall be referred to as simply as the 50th Regiment.

The early years of Hill's career from 1778

Hill's initial military experiences were one of adjustment to army life as it was a quiet period in the regiment's history, from a slow start in France and camps in the South West of England and Gibraltar, Hill found himself participating in the most widely documented wars of the Peninsular campaign.

Britain had been struggling against the French, since 1792, during the French revolution of 1789-1799 and then against Napoleon. Spain, Naples, Great Britain and the Netherlands joined Austria and Prussia in the first Coalition (1792–1797), the first major concerted effort of multiple European powers to contain Revolutionary France. The Emperor Napoleon, having made himself master of the continent was credited of designing a plan of massing all the European navies, to defeat England. Napoleon would not be defeated finally until 1815.

What follows here is a list of the battles and Skirmishes that involve Charles Hill; it is not intended to be a comprehensive account but allows for the reader to associate famous names, events and battles with the owner of our humble farm in Quinton.

Calvi 1794

In January 1794, Admiral Hood sought a new base for operations in the Mediterranean and set sail with the 50th Regiment on board. Corsica's harbours were of enormous value to the British fleet and the 50th anchored in the Bay of Martello and launched an attack on 17th February and took Bastia in a siege, which had the combined forces of both the Army and navy personnel.

The now eminent Captain Horatio Nelson was dispatched to settle plans for the landing of troops on Calvi. He took ships, which included H.M.S. Agamemnon (Holloway 7), and men, including the 50th Regiment on this mission. The regiment are proud to acknowledge the legend that exists today which claims that the regiment had served 'under Nelson', "it is true that the 50th were briefly transported in ships of Nelson's squadron, some indeed may well have been on board H.M.S. Agamemnon" (Holloway 9). However, Nelson was never in command of the entire expedition and the 50th like every other unit was under General Stuart's command throughout.

The plan was for the main attack to go in at dawn under cover of fire from the two batteries close to Mozello, which were erected the previous night. The 50th had the task of building one of these batteries and they worked through the night to complete it but there are no details of Hill's individual involvement. The two-pronged attack was a success and the capitulation of Calvi took place on 10th August 1794. It was during this attack on Calvi on 12th and 13th July 1794 that several British guns were destroyed (Holloway 9) The campaign was a major success but, during the attack on Calvi, Nelson was blinded in the right eye by stone splinters from a parapet struck by an enemy shell. Despite his injury, he returned to duty the following day. As a commander, he was known for the occasional disregard of orders from his seniors. This defiance brought him victories at the Battle of Copenhagen four years later, where he ignored orders to cease action by putting his telescope to his blind eye and claiming he could not have seen the signal to withdraw.

Egypt
1800-1804

The excitements of Corsica were followed by some uneventful years but in 1800 the 50th under Lt-Col Rowe arrived in Malta to join with *Sir Ralph Abercromby who was preparing to expel or capture the French army which Napoleon had left in Egypt. By now, there was a tension not only with the enemy but also within the English Naval and Military commanders. This tension prevented a swift attack on Cadiz, which was delayed as Abercromby's troops rehearsed disembarkation drills in preparation of the invasion repeatedly. The attack did eventually take place and ironically, in spite of his caution and rehearsals for a perfect attack, Abercromby was mortally wounded.

The 50th, in the brigade commanded by General Doyle, began the march to Cairo on 7th May 1801; conditions were appalling and the heat debilitating being 120°f in the shade. The soldiers lived in terror of the plague and were afflicted by dysentery and Opthalmia. The 50th obtained the nickname of 'the blind half hundred' from the amount of men who suffered from Opthalmia in this campaign. "It is interesting to note that on the capitulation of Cairo, a return gives the number of men of the English army who had lost their sight from that disease on that date as 160 while 200 had lost one eye" (Fyler 93).

On 21st June 1801, Hutchinson along with 4,500 British troops and with 25,000 Turks arrived at the outskirts of Cairo where, given the numbers involved it comes as no surprise that the French surrendered.

By the 16th July 1801 the 50th were back in Alexandria under orders to create a major diversion for Major General Coote on the eastern side of the city whilst Coote successfully attacked the their right side. The fighting continued over a period of ten days until again the French surrendered and were finally evacuated from Egypt. This concluded one of "the most competently conducted campaigns in the history of the British army" (Holloway 12) and they received new colours bearing the symbol of the Sphinx and the battle honour EGYPT for the parade in Cork in 1804.

1804 REGIMENTAL COLOUR

Figure 8 Colours bearing the Sphinx and the battle honour EGYPT.

The Peninsular

Histories of the peninsular war fall into two quite distinctive categories: the fully comprehensive text with detailed accounts of terrain, location, detailed military positions and personnel details and then a succinct factual account on manoeuvres, geography and deaths. In order to make some sense of Hill's involvement, there is an element of each here. The comprehensive work is from Fyler and Glover and the contextual information comes from Digby Smith, all of which are valuable sources for further information. There are no flawless accounts of historical events and the historian must check with other sources before using them as impeccable evidence.

In Hill's case, all the information on his medals and actions have been confirmed by Col. H.B.H. Waring O.B.E. regiment curator.

Copenhagen 1807

The Emperor Napoleon, having made himself master of the continent was credited of designing a plan of massing all the European navies to defeat England.

The British in an attempt to prevent Napoleon on his mission aimed to capture the Danish fleet to stop Napoleon gaining control of the same.

Initially the British government hoped to secure the position of the Danish fleet by peaceful means, but eventually abandoned that view and deciding to attack Copenhagen. The Second Battle of Copenhagen, (The First Battle of Copenhagen took place in 1801) which lasted from 16th August to the 5th September 1807 began in a swift and ruthless action, without any declaration of war. The Navy succeeded, but left behind a single frigate, which had previously been given as a gift to the Danes. Fyler describes the spectacular strength of the attack.

a battery built on piles at the entrance of the canal, an arsenal and harbour, mounting 68 guns, besides mortars; another pile battery in front of the citadel, mounting 86 guns and 9 mortars; and the citadel, which mounted 20 guns and 12 mortars. There were also block ships, floating batteries, and from 25 to 30 gunboats, all ready for action, whilst in the arsenal lay a fleet of 16 sail of the line and 21 frigates and sloops, besides three 74's on the stocks, one being nearly ready for launching (Fyler 94).

Figure 9 Copenhagen.
Copenhagen on fire because of British bombardment in 1807.
Painting by C.W. Eckersberg.

In 1807, Charles Hill now a Major, sailed for Copenhagen to take part in this campaign and landed at Charlotte Land, near the capital, on 16th August. The 50th was brigaded with the 32nd and 82nd regiments of foot under Major General Spencer and formed part of the 2nd Brigade of the 2nd Division under Lieutenant-General Sir David Baird. Major General Spencer's brigades marched into Copenhagen; Hill had commanded the pickets who drove in and pursued the enemy.

At daybreak on the 17th August, the three British columns marched in to Copenhagen and were attacked by the Danes; the Danish gunboats cannonaded them with grape and round shot. Many skirmishes took place over the next few days as the British army took the foundry and the cannon depot.

On the 24th of August the British army took posts on the heights around the town, the enemy's pickets were driven in and the Brigade of Guards occupied the summits. Sir D. Baird's division, to which the 50th Regiment belonged, took a redoubt (a temporary fortification built to defend a position such as a hilltop) which the enemy had been constructing for some time. Meanwhile, the enemy set parts of the suburbs of the town on fire. On the 26th, the enemy's gunboats made an attack on the left of the regiments' position and an unsuccessful sortie was attempted, but on the 29th August another attack on Wellesley's division resulted in many men being taken prisoner and the loss of provisions and cannon.

At this time most of the Danish army under the Crown Prince was defending the southern border against possible attack from the French; thus, the defence of Copenhagen was extremely limited. British troops commanded by General Wellesley defeated weak Danish forces near the town of Kage, south of Copenhagen. Within a few days, Copenhagen was completely encircled. The British offered to accept surrender, which was declined, so a British fleet under Admiral James Gambier bombarded the city from the 2nd September to the 5th September 1807. On 7 September 1807, Danish General Peymann surrendered both the city and the fleet.

Fyler sets the scene for the 50th Regiment:

They [the 50th] were promptly engaged and repulsed by the piquets of the 50th Regiment, commanded by Lieutenant Light; which, arousing all the other piquets, the enemy was compelled to retire with losses. General Baird, commanding the division, was twice wounded in the above, but did not quite the field. Lieutenant Light was promoted to a company for his conduct in the affair. The mortar and other batteries having been completed, the place was surrounded on the 1st Of September on the 7th they capitulated (98)… "The loss of the 50th consisted of Captain Coote killed, Major Charles Hill and Captain J.N Wilson wounded, and 2 sergeants, 2 corporals, 1 drummer, and 38 privates either killed or died of wounds. They captured a standard, pole, and box, which were borne by a sergeant between the colours during succeeding campaigns (108).

The regiment made a temporary camp and remained in place until the 23rd September, during which time the convention of Cintra stopped further hostilities. Colonel G.T Walker having obtained leave of absence after the battle of Vimiero, the command of the regiment devolved to Major Charles Napier who had joined from the Second Battalion to replace Major Charles Hill – severely wounded. After the above action, fifteen volunteers from the French 70th Regiment joined the 50th, and their long red plumes were worn as trophies by the band of regiment (Fyler.109).The regiment returned with the rest of the army to England and landed in Deal in November 1807 (98). By the end of the year, Britain was free from the immediate fear of invasion but Napoleon still sought to stifle British trade and the main ports were closed to her to prevent trade with Portugal.

The 50th Regiment of Foot in the Peninsular, 1807

Charles did not remain at home for long as the 1st Battalion embarked under sealed orders at Portsmouth on 17th December 1807, under the command of Major General George Townsend Walker. Among this nine thousand strong army was a thousand or more from the 50th Regiment of foot, complete with their ration of six wives, chosen at ballot per every hundred men (Holloway. 14).There appears to be no records to suggest Ann was one of the chosen wives, it would have either have been a wise decision not to enter the ballot or fate's kind hand in her favour.

The assembled men formed part of a brigade upwards of 1,000 men, consisting of the 29th, 32nd, 50th, and 82nd regiments, commanded by Major General Sir Brent Spencer.
As a result of severe storms in the Bay of Biscay they arrived badly battered and scattered, some of the vessels having turned back to Plymouth. The rest of the regiment eventually assembled in Gibraltar, and sailed to Cadiz in May 1808, where there was some action at the harbour but no damage or loss of life was recorded. The regiment landed at Porto St. Mary's and had a week on shore before sailing to Portugal on July 22nd, landing at Pigueras at the mouth of the Mondego River.

The 50th was brigaded with the 45th and 91st regiments and commanded by General J. Catlin-Crawford*. The first skirmish with the enemy took place at Brilos, near Obidos, on 1st August 1808, followed quickly by another on the 17th August. That same day the British Army under Sir Arthur Wellesley advanced against the strong position, which General La Borde had taken up at Rorica. On that occasion the central attack, under Sir Arthur Wellesley himself, (later granted the title the Duke of Wellington), was composed of General Hill's, Nightingale's* and Fane's brigades, with J Caitlin-Crawford's brigade (which included the 50th regiment) in reserve.

The clash that followed was the first action of any note in Wellesley's Portuguese campaign action. The British lost 441 men, the French lost 1,500 men and 300 French were captured, the battle on 21st August (was Wellesley's last campaign action of this year. Sir Harry Burrard (Wellesley's senior) forbade any offensive action by Wellesley who had now moved on to Vimiero to cover the disembarkation of troops. Burrard compelled Wellesley to stay in Vimiero. On that morning, the 43rd and 50th regiments under the command of General Lane, along with 95th Rifle Corps, discovered the enemy. At 7.00 am, the French advanced their horsemen, which could be seen to the south and General Fane's brigade resting in a churchyard occupied the centre of Vimiero Hill.

The French advanced on the Torres Vedras road. The 2nd, 3rd, 4th and 8th Brigades with 60th Rifles, four companies of the 95th and the 50th Regiment, under command of General Fane, moved across the ravine from the right to the left range of heights, leaving only the 1st Brigade on the right range.

The ground between the French and English armies was so wooded and broken, that after the French had passed the ridge where they had first been, no exact view of their movements could be recorded. French Generals Loisson and La Borde now formed one initial and two secondary attacks against Vimiero Hill, which the 50th was holding.

According to Wellesley's records, the attack was held amongst Olive trees, vineyards and Chestnut trees, all at a great height, with no water (Holloway.15). Captain Thomas Snow of the 50th went on a piquet and came under heavy fire – Captain Cooke was shot through the heart and Captain Snow became detached from his men in the woods, leaving Lieutenant Mark Rudkin in command. Rudkin gave orders to retire and the piquet's extending to the right and left fell back under a shower of bullets, Charles Hill was commanding one of these pickets and was wounded. Taking advantage of the protection given by the trees the 50th fired and retreated, eventually gaining some ground and found themselves in advance of the rest of the battalion. Their fire contributed to diverting the attention of the enemy from the main battalion, putting them in an advantageous position to cover passage into the town. Many more clashes and skirmishes continued over the next few days, but the regiment held their position on the hill until General Loisson directed his main column, upwards of 5,000 men, against the hill where the English numbered less than 900 men. The French complete with seven cannons marched towards the hill and attacked the 50th Regiment, "they attacked quickly and in number" (Fyler.105), Colonel Walker thinking there was no time to be lost, ordered an immediate volley and charge. The result was better than he had hoped for as the regiment had broken the angle at which the French were attacking and this created great confusion" and the threatening mass of men became an "ungovernable mob (106) says Fyler. The enemy retreated in an eastward direction away from their resources.

Digby Smith says, "This battle was another classic of 'column versus line' with the inevitable outcome when the line was the British Infantry" (267). The result of this "success" to the army (including the assistance derived from 20th Light Dragoons in their retreat) was 1000 enemy killed, 360 prisoners, and 6 pieces of cannon. The regiment not having more than 900 men in the field played its part in contributing to this victory. Meanwhile, General Anstruther repulsed a further attack on him and after fierce and bloody hand-to-hand combat drove the French back in disordered masses, but Colonel Taylor, pursuing them became entangled amongst the vineyards and the French turned on him and charged in superior numbers. He was overthrown and the English lost half their number and their Colonel.

Fyler sets the scene. "As far as the eye could reach, over the thickly planted valley with access to open country lying beyond the forest, the fugitives were running in wild disorder, their white sheepskin knapsacks discernable among the distant woods" (107).The ground was thickly strewed with muskets, side arms, accoutrements, and well-filled knapsacks, which had been hastily flung away" (108).

The loss of the 50th Regiment consisted of:

Captain Cooke killed.

Major Charles Hill and Captain T.N. Wilson wounded.

2 sergeants, 2 corporals, I drummer and 38 privates wounded and died of their wounds.

They also captured the Standard pole.

Next morning General Sir Hew Dalrymple arrived from Gibraltar and assumed command. There followed the notorious Convention of Cintra by which the French, their weapons, artillery, baggage and some of their plunder, were returned to France on British ships (Digby Smith 267). Wellesley had not condoned the agreement and signed it under pressure from General Sir Hew Dalrymple and Sir Harry Burrard, the former being keen to implicate Wellesley after the event. Wellesley sent his dispatches, which were received on 1st September. The public believed the peninsular was as good as liberated and guns were fired in the tower of London to celebrate. "Vimiero was the first significant victory that British troops had won on the Continent for more than half a century" (Glover 70). The battle of Vimiero marked the end of the first phase of the Peninsular War: but the convention of Cintra, which allowed Juno's army to leave Portugal in good order, was thought in England to be disgraceful, more so when they discovered the agreement had taken place on 22nd August and Dalrymple failed to disclose it until the 3rd September. The disparity between the accounts and the convention received great criticism and all the Generals were court-martialled but Wellesley was cleared of any wrong doing. "Before the storm died down more news came from the Peninsular. The British Army had been driven to its ships" (Glover.71).

Writing home after Vimiero a Doctor admitted that "to several a simple inspection of their wounds with a few words of consolation, or perhaps a little opium was all that could be recommended" (Glover 37). Surgical operations were almost as dangerous as the enemies weapons, as gangrene frequently set in. If the men were able to escape wounds their fears lay with catching malaria as it was rife and untreatable, with bizarre cures ranging from being doused with freezing cold water to drinking a bottle of Madeira per day!

On 23rd August 1808, the Regiment, including Hill were marching once again, this time into the peninsular war 1808 – 1814. These campaigns were a grueling series of struggles, which strained the resources of all the major participants. The resulting battles were not the easy victories that are often imagined today, and on various occasions, all of the major combatants suffered defeats and lost opportunities.

The battle at Fuentes De Onoro took place from the 3rd-5th May 1811, in the valley of the Rio de Casas, 27 km west of the fortress of Ciudad Rodrigo close to the Portuguese border. "It was an Anglo Portuguese victory over the French" (Digby Smith 358).The starving army of Portugal had since departed the area and conditions were considered so bad by Wellesley that he considered that they would not come back until the autumn. However, Major Massena of France had alternative ideas. He cobbled together a resilient group of men in high spirits and attacked Almeida, the attack was thwarted by Wellesley's decisive actions, and Massena withdrew.

The 50th had been supporting the 71st and 92nd here and on the afternoon of 3rd they formed on the right of the Duas Casas river. Five battalions picked from the 1st and 3rd divisions were driven from the lower parts of the village and with great difficulty held the upper parts; the position became critical and a gallant charge of combined regiments attacked the village of Fuentes De Onoro, which was built on the slope of the ravine. The attack resulted in them taking and holding their position in the French position. It appears likely through geography and the chronology of events that Charles Hill was captured at this juncture. There is little written about Hill's capture in Fyler's book other than a passing reference, where he says on the 13th June 1811 Charles Hill was made Lieutenant Colonel, he fought in this campaign and was taken prisoner. Glover reveals that Wellesley was not pleased with the events of battle of Fuentes de Onoro and expressed this opinion to the Secretary of State, calling it difficult (Glover. 155).

Dispatches

Hill was worthy of mention in Wellington's dispatches: these documents give a fascinating insight into the nature of operations in the Peninsular and Waterloo Campaigns during the Napoleonic Wars. They also reveal a thoughtful yet demanding Arthur Wellesley, whose many concerns as commander-in-chief included the needs of his officers, the feeding of his men and endless negotiations with British, Spanish and Portuguese leaders.

It is suggested that Wellington corrected notes or attached corrections for public or political inspection back in England, the result being there were two accounts being posted back to England.

**Figure 10 Sir Arthur Wellesley
The Duke of Wellington.**

The 1811 Campaign — Fuentes De Onoro.

In a letter from Lieut. General Viscount Wellington, K.B., to the Earl of Liverpool, Secretary of State' Villa Fermosa, 8th May, 1811.

"…The enemy's efforts on the right part of our position, after it was occupied as I have described above, were confined to a cannonade, and to some charges with his cavalry, upon the advanced posts. The regiments of the 1st division, under Lieut Colonel Hill of the 3rd Regiment of Guards, repulsed one of these; but as they were falling back, they did not see the direction of another in sufficient time to form to oppose it, and Lieut Colonel Hill was taken prisoner, and many men were wounded, and some taken, before a detachment of the British cavalry could move up to their support" (Dispatches 3).

The French claimed victory because they forced Wellington to relinquish 3 miles of ground at Fuentes De Onoro and drove the English back into confusion. The British also claimed victory because the village of Fuentes was in their hands and the French retired.

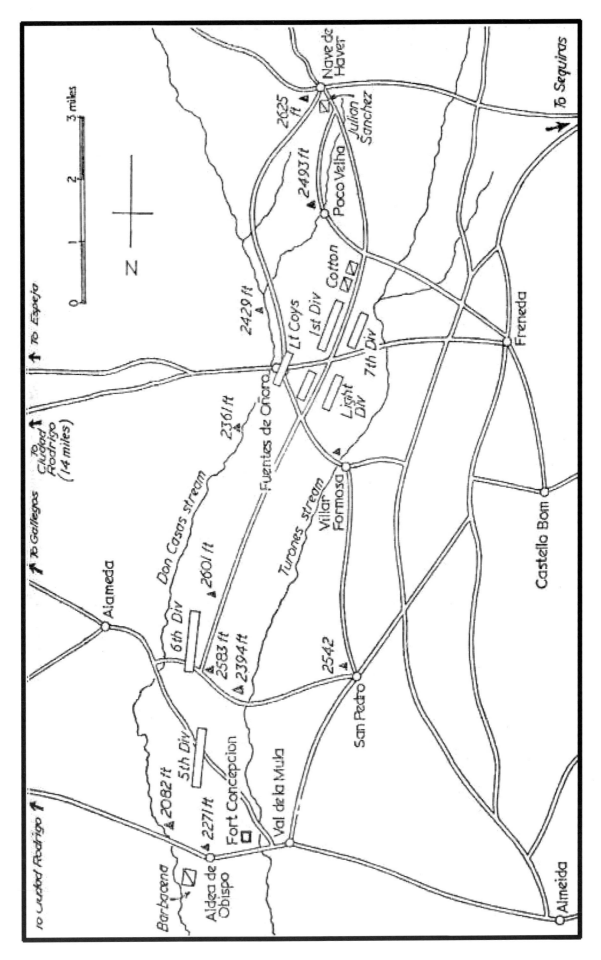

Figure 11 Fuentes do Onoro, position of Allied troops on 3rd May 1811.

The Battle of Vittoria

The battle of Vittoria was the final campaign and the most decisive of all the Peninuslar War battles; it was the last major battle against Napolean's forces in Spain and opened the way for the British forces under Wellington to invade France.

By mid 1812, the campaign in Spain had been going well for Wellington but the British forces suffered a serious setback at the siege of Burgos in September and October of 1812. Drunkenness was rife and discipline broke down, hundreds of Wellington's men were left floundering in the mud to die or to be taken prisoner by the French and those that survived were finally forced to retreat to Ciudad Rodrigo, a 16th and 17th walled town dating from the Roman Empire, which was frequently fought over. Glover says:

> "In and around Vitoria there was chaos, the streets were jammed with carriages, wagons, guns, and timbers. Into this confusion, Wellington launched the Hussars Brigade and swept around the north of the city spreading consternation and panic. The drivers cut the traces and rode off on their teams leaving the road blocked with guns" (Glover 155).

Despite this, the British forces soon recovered. After a winter spent preparing for battle, Wellington's Army was in a good condition, reinforcements had arrived, and 52,000 of them were British, so for once they were short of neither supplies nor men, therefore, Wellington was confident and they were ready by the spring of 1813 to go on the offensive. The pressure was intense as expectations of a successful campaign were high in Britain.

The situation in the French Army was far different. Napoleon recalled 15,000 veteran French troops needed for the upcoming campaign in Germany. Meanwhile Spanish Guerrillas were busy trying to destroying French morale and Napoleon's famed spy network was failing, leading Napoleon to believe the forces under Wellington were much fewer and in much poorer condition than in reality.

The advance began on May 22nd 1813: Wellington pressed forwards with all his divisions, steadily in spite of the difficult terrain, towards Vittoria. The early stages of the campaign went well with Wellington's army in two wings advancing and retaking Salamanca with little difficulty. By the 13th June, Wellington's forces had forced the French to abandon the fortress of Burgos, which they blew up as they fled. Wellington decided to advance via a very rugged and mountainous region, which proved to be highly successful. The French disregarded any possibility that Wellington would advance via the mountains which shows how badly they misjudged him. Wellington's plan was to cross the Ebro, which would allow him to use the port of Santander. A few brief engagements followed on the 18th June as the French realised that Wellington had outflanked them and then on the 20th of June, Wellington halted to concentrate his army and make final plans for the upcoming battle. French prisoners held captive told him how chaotic the enemy's army was, adding to Wellington's confidence of victory.

On a bleak, wet miserable day at daybreak on the 21st June, the battle of Vittoria began, "The basin in which the French had taken up position was eight miles broad by ten long" (Fyler 153).The French army numbered 60,000 with 153 guns and deployed in a rough "L" shape. The Anglo-Portuguese and Spanish army had 78,000 men and 96 guns, which Wellington spilt into four columns with the centre two under his personal command totaling 30,000 men. His plan was to hit the French line in several places. Within an hour, the French position was under threat as Spanish troops took the entrance to the heights of Puebla threatening the French left flank. General Hill's brigade, who was separated by a high ridge from the British, both at centre and left positions and was ordered to force the passage of the Zadora, beyond the Puebla defile. This resulted in General Hill's Brigade taking advantage of the height, thus drawing off more than two whole French divisions from the main line, more than Wellington could have hoped for. It was not quite so easy everywhere for Wellington; General Graham attacking the French right flank at the crossing of the Zadorra River, north of Vittoria had run into determined opposition at the village of Gamara Mayor. Wellington was becoming concerned, as by noon his centre columns under Picton and Dalhousie had not yet arrived. When they finally arrived, Picton, impatient for orders, led his division to take the bridge of Mendoza. By the afternoon, the French had been driven from the heights and were being squeezed into the area around Vittoria as the allies drove at them from the centre and the left flanks. The French were now under threat from both flanks and the centre with an artillery duel between 75 allied guns and 76 French guns; this being the biggest artillery battle of the war and the largest amount of artillery Wellington would have command of until Waterloo. Wellington prepared for the final stroke, outflanked and under pressure, the French finally broke and began to retreat.

Figure 12 Regiment at the battle of Vittoria by Brian Palmer.

The 87th Regiment defend the walls against the French 13th Dragoons as they charge by during the Battle of Vittoria.

The retreating French convoy contained much of King Joseph's 'court', who had indicated the road to Salvetiera as the line of retreat. Joseph's convoy contained 3,000 carriages and stretched for 12 miles by the time it reached Vittoria. The convoy was too large to escape the Allied troops who were eager for plunder. Among the French convoy were new wagons from France containing over 5 million gold francs! Equivalent to £8,197,200 based on current conversion rate of 0.792 pounds to euro (2008).

King Joseph himself escaped capture and left all his personal belongings in his flight. Looting was rife on both sides and Wellington only managed to retrieve a small part of the spoils. The Allies lost around 5,000 men; the French lost around 8,000 but also vast amounts of money, equipment, wagons, artillery guns and other treasures, but surprisingly no Imperial Eagles. The news of the defeat spread throughout Europe and Napoleon's old enemies Austrian, Russia and Prussia all pressed for war. Vittoria not only marked the end of French ambitions in Spain but the beginning of the end for Napoleon.

Lieutenant Colonel Charles Hill joined Wellington's allied armies at Vittoria, on the day of battle at a fortified city in Northern Spain where he commanded the regiment.

> At daybreak on June 21st, the battle of Vittoria began, the weather being rainy with a thick vapour. The British were separated from the 50th by a ridge and were ordered to force their way through and beyond. The skirmishes began and continued until the ridge was won.
> The Col-de-Maya was menaced by P'Erlon's men from Espalette and Urdax, furnishing 18,000 bayonets. The first Brigade marched into Elisonda on the 8th July and took up their position on an elevated ridge" […]"the 71st and 92nd regiments were camped near Maya to the left of the road to Urdax and Espalette and the 50th bivouacked among some trees about a mile to the right (Fyler 154).

On 25th July, P'Armagnac's division pushed back the English and Marensin's division attacked the 71st and 92nd regiments near the Passes. Lieutenant Cameron, seeing the difficulties, sent in the 50th regiment to their assistance. P'Armagnac's division were taken by surprise and driven clean out of the pass. Sir W. Napier, writing of this charge of the 50th, quotes,

> "that fierce and formidable old regiment, charging the head of an advancing column, drove it clear out of the pass of Lessenssa". They then joined the 34th regiment and these regiments poured a destructive fire on the advancing foe. The 50th Regiment then retired on the position taken up by the 92nd Regiment. In this position they were confronted by the enemy and the loss to the regiment over two charges, was severe, especially the grenadier company. Captain Ambrose, who commanded the regiment, was mortally wounded and calling his Sergeant gave him his sword, saying… "the enemy shall never have it". His Subaltern Lieutenant Deignton was also killed with his cap on his sword, cheering on the men" (161).

Lieutenant Colonel Hill of the 50th Foot Battalion commanded the first Battalion and was severely wounded in the groin by a spent bullet during the second charge and the temporary command of the regiment devolved on Major O.N. Campbell (Fyler. 161). He rejoined the 1st Battalion on the death of Colonel Stewart and commanded it at Vittoria and until wounded at Col-de-Maya"(Fyler) and his actions gained him a gold medal.

Curiously, the episode at Maya has, in the regiment's history, received less than its due attention. It was after all an unwelcome defeat after a long series of successes and Wellington, usually so generous and specific in his praise, refers in his dispatches briefly and almost as a formality to 'these brave troops' but for the grievously wounded Colonel Hill it was an undoubtly the pinnacle of a career of continuous distinction" (Holloway. 31).

The 50th arrived home rightly to be greeted as one of the most distinguished regiments in the British army and it was an experienced and confident body of men that later left for Jamaica.

The Years following the Peninsula war

Orders were received on 4th November 1818 for the Regiment to proceed to Jamaica, in accordance with which they left Dublin and headed to Cork, where they embarked on 7th and 8th January in the transports of "John", "Fame" and "Alfred".

They were detained by adverse winds until the 28th January 1819, on which date they sailed, arriving and disembarking in March. Their strength on landing was:

Field Officers 2, Captains 6, Subalterns 14, Staff 5, Sergeants 28, Drummers 20, Privates 608, Total 683.

"They were a splendid body of men when they reached Jamaica, and for 4 months continued in their usual health, but the season was unusually dry, hardly any rain falling until the end of July, to which is attributed the fearful mortality from yellow fever, which devastated the regiment, officers and men alike falling victims to the pestilence.

Among the deaths were many officers and men, who had served with honour in the Peninsular. The fatal progress of the disease was not checked until the end of the year, when more than half of the men, women and children had been laid in a grave.

The casualties from the disembarkation on the 8th March to the following December is as follows:

Colonel Hill CB commanding.

Captain and Brevit-Major Rowe.

Captain and Brevit-Major Montgomery.

Lieutenant Richardson.

Lieutenant North.

Ensign Batlow.

Ensign Edwards.

Ensign Harley.

Paymaster Montgomery.

Lieutenant and Adjutant Lyon.

Assistant Surgeon Bourn,

255 Sergeants, drummers, privates, besides women and children.

*Colonel Charles Hill CB who was wounded in Vimiero and who commanded the regiment at Vitoria was still suffering from the effects of wounds and had been advised to remain in England, but he would not leave the regiment in which he had served so long" (Fyler 193).

Holloway also recorded Hill, he says "within six months Hill himself half the men of his battalion and more than half their accompanying women and children were dead. Yellow fever had succeeded where Junot, Marmont, and Soult had failed" (34).

Charles died of yellow fever on 31st August 1819 whilst remaining with his regiment. We now have a dramatic account of some of the battles, tactics and plundering that took place during Hill's career, we can conclude that the man died with honour in defence of his duty and beyond.

A letter from the War Office
13th June 1820 to King

"It is most humbly submitted for your majesty's

approbation by the Secretary of War, that in consideration

of generous conduct of the late Colonel Charles Hill of the

50th Regiment of Foot, who on 31st August 1819 fell as a

victim to the yellow fever at Jamaica while attending the

sick of the regiment he commanded, at the time when no

other soldier of the corps could be persuaded to enter the

hospital, a royal Bounty of two hundred pounds a year be

granted to Mrs Anne(sic) Hill in view of the pension

allowed to her as widow of the above-mentioned officer, the

same to commence from 1st September 1819.

George

Figure 13 Letter from King George 3rd.

This was signed by George
but as George 3rd was very ill at the time,
it was the Prince Regent who dealt with these affairs.

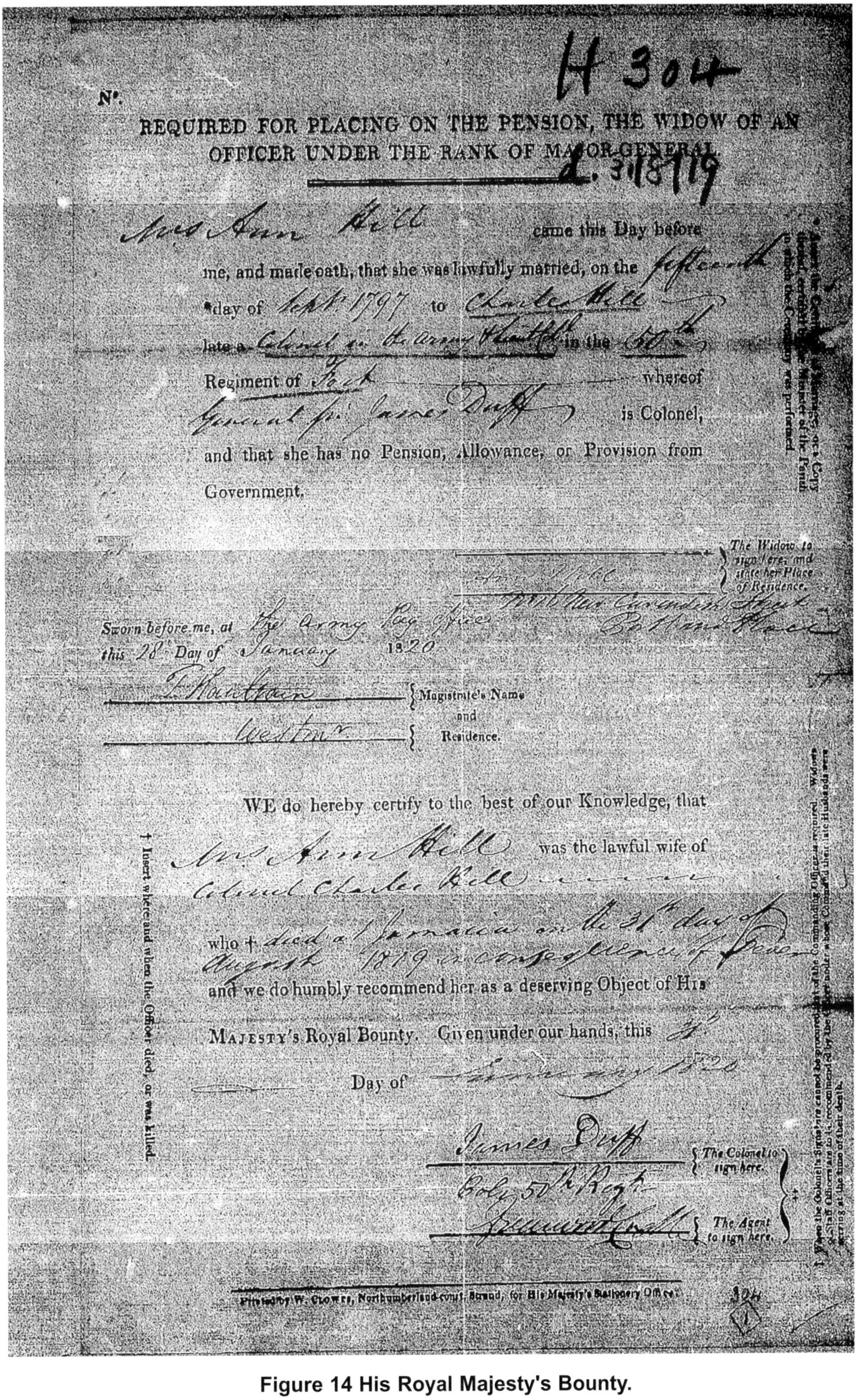

H 304

No.

REQUIRED FOR PLACING ON THE PENSION, THE WIDOW OF AN OFFICER UNDER THE RANK OF MAJOR-GENERAL.

d. 31/8/19

Mrs Ann Hill came this Day before me, and made oath, that she was lawfully married, on the fifteenth *day of Septr 1797 to Charles Hill late a Colonel in the Army & Lieut Col in the 50th Regiment of Foot whereof General Sir James Duff is Colonel, and that she has no Pension, Allowance, or Provision from Government.

* Annex the Certificate of Marriage, or a Copy thereof, certified by the Minister of the Parish in which the Ceremony was performed.

Ann Hill
No. 11 New Cavendish Street
Portland Place

The Widow to sign here, and state her Place of Residence.

Sworn before me, at the Army Pay Office
this 28th Day of January 1820

T. Hantham — Magistrate's Name
Westm^r — and Residence.

WE do hereby certify to the best of our Knowledge, that Mrs Ann Hill was the lawful wife of Colonel Charles Hill who † died at Jamaica on the 31st day of August 1819 in consequence of Fever and we do humbly recommend her as a deserving Object of His Majesty's Royal Bounty. Given under our hands, this 31st Day of January 1820

† Insert where and when the Officer died, or was killed.

James Duff — The Colonel to sign here.
Col^y 50th Reg^t
Greenwood & Cox — The Agent to sign here.

‡ Where the Colonel's Signature cannot be procured, that of the Commanding Officer or of the Regiment, recommended by ... Officers ... serving at the time of their death.

Printed by W. Clowes, Northumberland-court, Strand, for His Majesty's Stationery Office.

304

Figure 14 His Royal Majesty's Bounty.

Promotions and medals

The Regimental battalions were divided into 10 companies with a Lieutenant Colonel, 2 Majors, and 10 Captains – none of these officers would have received any formal training as that was reserved for the engineers and the artillery. Only one officer in twenty was promoted through the ranks, normal promotion was by seniority rather than merit, but a rich man, whom Charles presumably was, providing he had served a minimum period in his rank, could buy his next promotion. A regiment was an administrative unit and the basic fighting unit was the battalion. Most regiments had at least two battalions and Charles was with the 1st Battalion (usually but not always) of 50th Regiment of Foot, occasionally there was a small single battalion regiment. A battalion was supposed to have a full strength up to 1000 men, ten companies of 100 each but often on campaign, due to casualties, disease and a shortage of recruits, it meant that battalions often went into battle with as few as 500 troops. Through promotion or purchase, Charles went up through the ranks from 27th December 1778 to 3lst August 1819.

The regimental records of Hill's promotions.
Hill, Colonel. Charles, C.B.

27th December 1778 Ensign.

13th October 1780 Lieutenant.

17th February 1794 Captain, Lieutenant and Captain.

25th September 1803 Battalion Major.

1st August 1804. Major.

25th July 1810. Battalion Lieutenant Colonel.

13th June 1811 Lieutenant Colonel.

12th August 1819 Battalion Colonel.

31st August 1819 Dies. His marriage lasted 23 years and he served the army for 41 years.

Spent most of his early service at home.
Active service:-
Peninsula- Present at Roleira and wounded at Vimiero, while commanding the picquets.
Commanded 2 Bn. 50th 1810-12
Rejoined 1st Bn on death of Col. Stewart and commanded it at Vittoria and until wounded at Col de Maya, 25/7/1813, by a spent bullet in the groin and shortly afterwards being hit on the forehead (P.p.330). (Unfortunately, there is no indication as to the book it was referring to).
He rejoined at Toulouse.
Gold Medal for Vittoria*.
Copenhagen 1807. Commanded a picquet during the sortie.
Died at Fort Augusta, Jamaica of yellow fever, whilst in command of the 50th,
31/8/1819, aged 57, having served 41 years in the Regt.
Information supplied by Col H.B H Waring. O.B.E. Curator

Although many commanding officers of various campaigns were given medals to commemorate a particular campaign or battle, the modern era of campaign medals did not start until 1816 with the authorization of the Waterloo Medal for the services of the previous year. Charles received: three medals during his career.

The first was a gold medal for Vittoria in 1813 whilst in the 1st Battalion 50th Regiment of Foot as Lieutenant Colonel. Secondly The Hot Shot Medal, for taking part in the defeat of the Spanish during the siege of Gibraltar on 13th September 1782.

The Medal yearbook reads

"Obverse. A moored floating battery with three fire bombs landing on the roof. Below which is inscribed in two lines. "The Pastora Ship/ Adml Morino .On a third line is the recipients' name.

Reverse. An active furnace with "Fur " to the left of it and "nace" to the right. Below, is the inscription in five lines.

Spaniards defeated by RED hot SHOT at GIBRALTAR /Sept ry 1782. Both obverse and suspender are edged with a cable border.

Size 38mm

Metal-Copper, one known in silver.

Suspension. Flat suspender fitted to the top with a hole in the centre through which either cord or ribbon was threaded.

Named medals are known to: T, Cole. T, Dodd. J, Hamilton. C, Hills*. H, Hillson. H, Hobbs. J, Rogers. J, Shaw. J, Wheatley. (silver).

The grand attack, which started on the 13th September 1782, was opened by a cannonade from 200 pieces of heavy ordnance, followed by an assault of some 40,000 Frenchmen, under the Duc de Crillon, from the landward side.

The bay was crowded with combined French and Spanish fleets composed of forty-seven line-of-battle ships, numerous frigates, small armed vessels and ten battery ships which their designer, the French engineer Jean Claude d,Arcon, states cost over half a million pounds apiece. They were a converted line-of battle-ships from 600.-1,400 tons, armed with nine to twenty-one guns, with crews of from 350 to 760 men. The fronts of the batteries were protected by thick layers of square timber and covered with a sloping roof. The whole was lined with cordage and hides. In order to make them fireproof, a reservoir was installed in each battery from which, by means of hand pumps could be kept wet. Each battery had a single sail to enable it to take up its designed position, which was about four hundred yards off shore.

The fate of these batteries, in view of the high hopes that they raised, became comical. The wetting system was so efficient that not only did it keep the fabric wet but all the powder as well, so that by the time the two leading and largest batteries, the Talla Piedra and Pastora, had got into position they were more like soaking targets than fireproof batteries.

During the first evening of the attack a red-hot shot became lodged in and set alight to the roof of the Talla Piedra, on which D,Arcon was serving, but as the fire was so severe it could not be moved".

In the Medal yearbook 2001, the hot shot medal is featured and the named medals are listed. "C. Hills" is one of them and the "s" on the end of Hill is an error in the inscription. It has been checked with the Regimental Museum record to ensure it is the correct 'Hill'. The medal yearbook gives an illustration of the medal with descriptions of both sides.

Finally, his third medal was British Order of Chivalry. Order of the Bath, founded in 1725. The most honourable Order of the Bath, established by King George I,

The Military Division had three classes:
Knight Grand Cross (G.C.B.)
Knight Commander (K.C.B.)
Companion CB, It was later reorganized after the Napoleonic Wars (which Charles received).

The Hot Shot Medal

Figure 15 The Hot Shot Medal.

Regimental Colours

This illustration of the colours, taken from Colonel Fylers book The Queens Own, was used throughout the Peninsular War. In 1804, new colours for the Regiment were received and the old colours were burnt with military honours. The picture was taken at the Herald's College, to which the following note from Major Haven, commanding the Regiment at the time was attached: "The Colours were borne with honour in the campaigns of Copenhagen, Vimiero, and Corunna in the Walcheren Expedition and all through the Peninsular War"(289). Hill was involved in at least two of these campaigns.

Figure 16 The new Colours for the 50th Regiment.

Uniform for 50th Regiment

U. Pericoli in The armies of Waterloo in 1815 suggests that no records exist for the 50th Regiment's uniform, although there are many references for later years and some written accounts. In 1767, an order was issued directing the regimental number to be placed on all the buttons: the number was surmounted by a crown with single laurel leaves on the edge. In 1769 when Charles Hill joined as Ensign, the lapels or loops were changed to become square at equal distances, there was a red stripe to be added down the centre. Later on in 1770-1775 a breast-plate was added, brass for private, silver for the Officers.

Figure 17 The 50th (Queens Own) Regiment, 1850 dress uniform.

As the Regiment was initially only intended for the seven-year war, it has been difficult to find exact uniforms for Hill and as he progressed through various promotions. Regimental records vary enormously in the early years and there are some inconsistencies possibly due to rank or inadequate record keeping. However, records do improve over the years and although it would be wrong to state what Hill actually wore at any point these illustrations give us an indication of battle dress and dress uniform.

Private Soldier 50ᵗʰ REGᵗ
about 1740.
From Sketch in War Office Book.

FRONTISPIECE.

Figure 18 A Private in the 50th Regiment c1740.

Parish of Kingston.
1819 Jamaica

Mural tablet

In the cemetery of this parish lie interned the mortal remains of -

Col. Charles Hill, Lieut. Colonel of 50th Regiment of Foot, and a companion of the most Honourable Military Order of the Bath. As Major and afterwards as Lieut.Colonel of his regiment, he was himself eminently conspicuous in the numerous actions of the war in which it was engaged and assisted in placing on its Colours the glorious distinctions of Vimiero, Vitoria, Pyrenees and Peninsula. Covered with wounds and with honour, he might, at the peace, have retired to the enjoyment of his country's blessing and applause, but anxious to see his old regiment restored to it's wonted force and discipline, and then unwilling to quit it again, ordered on instant duty and an unfavourable change of climate, he ultimately fell a victim to his ever anxious solicitude for those with whom his blood had so often been shed, and together with a numerous band of his gallant officers and soldiers perished by a desolating fever on 3lst August 1819 in the 57th year of his age and the 41st of his military service.

This stone is erected to his memory by his affectionate wife Anne (sic) Hill.

Figure 19 Charles Hill's burial stone.

Taken from Monumental Inscriptions of Jamaica compiled by Philip Wright

Chapter Three

The end of an era as
The Hawthorn Farm is sold

Ann Hill survived her husband by many years, living in Connaught Place London until 1854. The farm having remained in the family from 1773 was now up for auction and held in a bitter dispute between Millar, Bond, Richard Aldridge and others, names of family and friends that appeared on her marriage licence and in either her will or that of her late husband.

The dispute was over the ownership of lands, the complications arose partially because her father's estate had not been wound up correctly and there was a distinct lack of proof of ownership. Additionally, the ownership and whereabouts of a painting of a Mr Miller was in dispute by another family member. Sadly, there are few details on the painting, other than what appears in the will, which mentioned in the deeds of Hawthorn house on Lot Four and Five.

The farm was sold in twelve lots and will now appear in that order for ease of reference. The details of the lots are listed as on the sale notice followed a brief account of what became of the land, which is not intended to be definitive or complete, there is always more to learn!

Some of the fields remained agricultural as they were encompassed by other farms, including, Windmill Farm, Bristnall Hall Farm, Cooper's Farm and Redhall Farm.

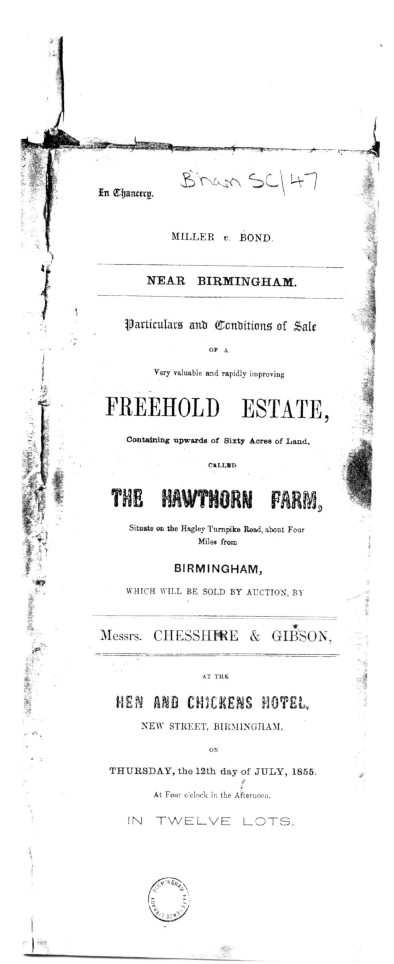

Figure 20 Particulars and conditions of sale 1855.

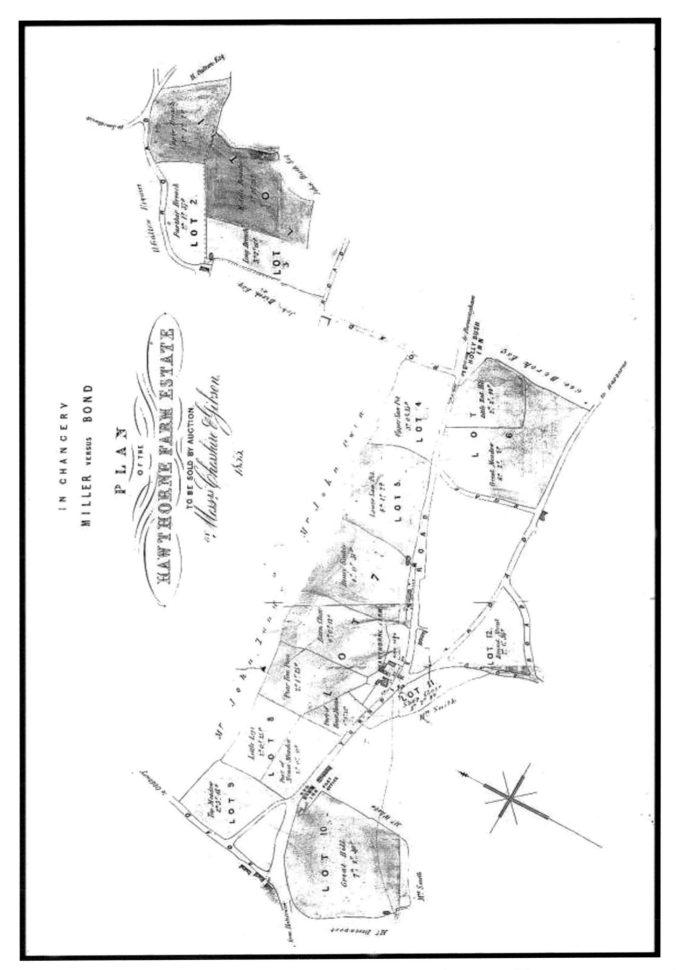

Figure 21 The plan of Hawthorn Farm 1855 (not to scale).

The Particulars of the sale

Lot One. Two fields of elevated land known as UPPER BREECH AND MIDDLE BREECH possessing very extensive views of The Lightwoods, King's Norton and Clent Hills, 8 acres, 0 roots, 27 poles.

Lot Two. A similar field of land adjoining lot 1, called the FATHER BREECH, possessing a very considerable frontage and containing 2 acres, 1 root and 37 poles.

Lot Three. Long Breech. A piece of land abutting upon the former lots, called LONG BREECH containing, 3 acres, 2 roots, 16 poles or thereabouts, the above lots are bounded by the estates of Mr Galton and Mr Birch.

Lot Four. A field of valuable land. Called the UPPER SAW PIT PIECE, fronting to the main Turnpike Road, at the 4 mile stone and to the road leading towards the Breeches, (sic) containing 3 acres or 35 poles or thereabouts.

Lot Five. A similar piece of land adjoining lot four, called the LOWER SAW PIT PIECE, containing 4 acres, 1 root, 2 poles or thereabouts.

Lot Six. Bounded by good roads on three sides, LITTLE RED HILL, GREAT MEADOWS.

Lot Seven. The Hawthorn farmhouse, buildings, and homestead. Fronting to the said Turnpike Rd, and several pieces or parcels of land adjoining thereto, known as THE HONEYSUCKLE, THE BARN, CLOSE, THE PEAR TREE PIECE AND PART OF HOUSE MEADOW. Containing 12 acres, 1 root, 0 poles or thereabouts, farmed by Mr Cooper.

Lot Eight. Two pieces of land, known as LITTLE LEYS and the remainder of the HOUSE MEADOW, also fronting to the Turnpike Road and containing 4 acres, 0 roots, 35 poles or thereabouts.

Lot Nine. A very valuable piece of land possessing a double frontage called the TOP MEADOW containing 2 acres, 3 roots, 18 poles or thereabouts.

Lot Ten. Called the GREAT HILL, situated on the rising ground leading up to the Quinton, on the said Turnpike Road, containing 7 acres, 1 root, 30 poles, or thereabouts.

Lot Eleven. Possessing a very long frontage to two roads, called SHOP CLOSE, containing 1 acre, 2 roots, 8 poles, or thereabouts.

Lot Twelve. Called ROUNDABOUT, and surrounded by good roads, containing 2 acres, 1 root, 36 poles or thereabouts.

Great tithe FREE, except as to lot six, but subject to small tithe and land tax

Lot One

Galton's Land

Two fields of elevated land known as Upper Breech and Middle Breach possessing very extensive views of The Lightwoods, King's Norton and Clent Hills
8 acres, 0 roots, 27 poles.
This became Castle Croft and the Wolverhampton Road, although there is little chance of a clear or extensive view to King's Norton these days. It was later subdivided, as were many of the plots, into two closes called Middle Breach and Little Breach by 1907.

Hubert John Barclay Galton purchased plots One, Two and Three of Hawthorn Farm when they went up for Auction in 1855, presumably because they adjoined his own substantial park in Warley where the family had built their home, Warley Abbey. He had inherited the land from his father Samuel Galton junior and he from his father before him, Samuel Senior. The park gardens were landscaped under Hubert's direction by London Architect Robert Lugar and built by Young and Sharpe, who completed the project in 1820.

Hubert Galton came from a fascinating family, spreading their interests and their businesses amongst the people of Birmingham and the surrounding area. Samuel Galton junior met regularly with The Lunar Society, a group of many famous names associated with the City of Birmingham. The group included; Matthew Boulton the industrialist, James Watt who gave us the steam engine, Erasmus Darwin physician and writer (Charles Darwin's Grandfather), William Herschel, who discovered the planet Uranus, John Baskerville, printer and designer, Dr Joseph Priestley, the chemist who discovered oxygen and Josiah Wedgwood, famous for his tableware (and the other grandfather of Charles Darwin), to name but a few. *The Lunar Society* held meetings during the late 1700s in each other's houses. The great minds met to exchange information about their work, scientific experiments, discoveries, opportunities that may present themselves and current topics. Named *The Lunar Society* as they met from 2 am until 8 am going home by the light of the moon in those pre street-lit days that we now all take for granted. The name has now re-emerged and thrives today in a modern format by providing a forum for its members and discusses the way *"forward"* for Birmingham on many issues.

In 1777, Samuel junior married Lucy Barclay of Barclays bank, the family that founded the Bank and lived on Hagley Row and then in Great Barr Birmingham. It was whilst living there that he decided to build the Warley Hall Estate, which included farms, houses and the Warley Tor building. There were moves to alter the "Tor", a simple building into a family home but this was rejected in favour of building Warley Abbey. Humphrey Repton drew up the plans for the transformation of the park in 1795 to include a grand house. He proposed "improvements", a fashionable pursuit at the time, which included pulling up all the estate hedging in order to create an eye-catching vista over the land.

Galton does not appear to have lived at the "Tor" for any great lengths of time but Dave Yates in, *A place in Time* suggests that a farm was not prestigious enough for him; it was not fitting for a gentleman of his standing to do so. Therefore, he probably stayed only when conducting business in the area. It was his son Hubert, that was the first to live on the land with his wife and family, Hubert had married his cousin Mary Barclay. They had four children, Mary Barclay Junior, Diana, Julia Theresa and Robert Cameron. Both Robert and Julia died at a very young age, followed by Diana at the age of 22. It was after her death that Hubert and Mary left the Abbey, presumably in grief. The sale deeds of the land record them as living in Bath and upon his death the estate went to his only surviving daughter Mary Barclay, September 1864.

The land was tenanted out to many families and individuals during Mary's ownership and as she was childless, she left the land to her two cousins Howard Douglas Leonard and Major Hubert George Howard Galton. The deeds describe all the lands and hereditments included in the Galton's property, which of course includes descriptions of the plots that were once part of Hawthorn Farm. They are described as plots One, Two and Three in 1855 and called Upper, Middle, Farther and Long Breech and are mentioned in the will by name. Also given to the brothers were the lands at Little Lightwoods and Great Lightwoods, land previously owned by the Lyttelton family and acquired by the Galton's in 1838.

Figure 22 Castle Road and the Wolverhampton Road c1950.
Part of the original farm, which became Galton's estate.

The original farm field names pop up again in 1909 when some of the remaining land was leased out to William Henry Millard of Hollyhurst on the Bristol Road in Birmingham. He paid £2,000 by way of mortgage at an interest rate of 4% per annum to be paid quarterly. It is evident that he sub leased much of the land to individuals and subsequently sold off the freeholds as the land was purchased for housing.

Lot Two

A similar field of land adjoining lot 1, called the Father Breech, possessing a very considerable frontage and containing 2 acres, 1 root and 37 poles.

**This became the School grounds, Castle Road East and Wolverhampton Road
N.B a footpath is claimed over these lots, as shown on the plan. The vendors do not admit this right but the lots are sold subject to it, if it exists.**

Figure 23 photograph entitled Castle Road to the Wolverhampton Road c1950.

It was interesting that this footnote above concerning the footpath was later tested upon, as many years later in 1923, an application was made at Worcestershire Quarter Sessions to move the footpath through the land. It had run through from Castle Road East through what is now Gateley Road on to what was Beech Lanes and is now Hagley Road West.

The item on the agenda was of the intention to move the footpath to the right of the lanes very slightly aligning up the lanes. Now of course the footpath has developed into roads taking you off the Hagley Road West up Gateley Road over the Wolverhampton Road up an alley along the houses to Castle Croft, where no rural lands now exists.

Castle Road School

Figure 24 Lightwoods School.

Opened as Castle Road School
In May 1908

School Log book

May 4th 1908

School opens with 79 scholars. The staff consists of Mary Cobb mistress Harriet Goode Jessie Jones assistant.

May 8th

There are 91 on the register and the average attendance is 86.I find that more than half of the children have not been to school before.

May 22nd

There are 116 on the books. Average 107, owing to the poor staff very little has been given yet to organisation, only a temporary timetable is being used. Mistress is spending her time with class 11, as there is no teacher for it.

May 24th 1908

I have been instructed to admit children in standard 1
Half holiday today; Empire day.

June 16th
    School opens. Miss Dorothy Lilly certificated assistant is added to the staff.

June 19th
    Average 128. I have been informed that the school year must end July 31st.

Report after visit of 14th October 1908

"This new Infants school was opened on 4th May 1908 in a suitably appointed building. There are nearly 200 names on the books including the children in standard one.
The scholars were found to be very backward upon admission. A skilfully planned scheme of work and timetable has been adopted. The institution proceeds on good lines and is very promising. Some pictures are much needed."

Staff Mary Eliz Cobb Head mistress
Dorothy Lilley certificated assistant"
Harriet Lucas Goode uncertificated"
Jessie Jones uncertificated"
Bertha Williams uncertificated
Gwendoline R Hipkiss P.J.
Signed; Sydney Benson

The school was surrounded by fields and most children came from nearby. There were only a few houses in Castle Road and Lightwoods Hill and most children walked to school from Frederick Road, Gateley Road, Beech Lanes, and Birch Road. Some children came from Bearwood, which was a longer trek and the logbook indicates that there was much emphasis placed on the weather as this affected the numbers attending. Records were exacting and considered of great importance.

Lot Three
Long Breech

A piece of land abutting upon the former lots, called Long Breech containing, 3 acres, 2 roots 16 poles or thereabouts, The above lots are bounded by the estates of Mr Galton and Mr Birch.

Later became Wolverhampton Road, Kenilworth Road and Warwick Road.

It is interesting to see the names, Kenilworth and Warwick appearing here as Ann Troughton prior to her marriage to Hill was called "Ann of Warton, Warwickshire " and Ann of Warwick in papers relating to her father and his business dealings, at a period of time when she lived in Kenilworth. The local council were unable to confirm the origin of these roads but it would seem to be rather a coincidence to be anything other than a reference to either Ann's early life or a reference to the family's domicile.

Howard Douglas Galton died on 25th July 1923 leaving the remaining parts of the estate to his brother Major Hubert George Galton. In an indenture, dated 21st August 1900 between Major H.G.H Galton and Birmingham City Corporation there was a grant of easement allowed on the land to lay the Elan valley water pipes going under the few properties at the time and under the fields.

The Galtons received £2000 compensation from Birmingham Corporation for "loss and inconvenience" whilst they put in pipes and conduiting across the land and requested access any time day or night to cleanse and inspect the pipes or to carry out repairs.

The family has certainly left their mark in the area giving their names to Galton Road, Barclay Road, Galton Canal Bridge, and Saint Hubert's Church. St Hubert's Catholic Church was built on the Wolverhampton Road after Major Galton left land and money to the diocese for that purpose, after the Galtons converted to Catholicism. Major Galton outlived his brothers so he inherited the land, which he subsequently left to his daughter. Tragically, she predeceased him, but the church was completed by 1935 and Galton's wishes were complied with and so it serves its Catholic community today.

Lots Four and Five
A piece of valuable land

Called the UPPER SAW PIT PIECE, fronting to the main Turnpike Road, at the 4-mile stone, and to the road leading towards the Breeches, (sic).

A similar piece of land
Adjoining, Called the LOWER SAW PIT PIECE, containing 4 acres,1 root, 2 poles or thereabouts.

Lot Five A similar piece of land adjoining lot four. Called the LOWER SAW PIT PIECE, containing 4 acres, 1 root, 2 poles or thereabouts.

These two lots became the Hawthorn Croft, Birch Hollow, Birch Lane and at least part of Dairy Court. This initially became the area known as The Hawthorns, Beech Lanes, comprising the roads that we now know as Hagley Road West, Birch Lane, Hawthorn Croft, Birch Holloway, Squirrels Holloway and Rose Avenue which appears to be the farm field border, although there is no clear demarcation. Stanley Road was a dividing field line which was not cut through as a road until the early to mid-1900s.

There is an awkward shaped gap in lots three and five here that belonged to another farm, it covered the area of Birch Road towards the main road and part of what became Dairy Court.

Mr John Owen and Mr Birch bought the land behind these fields in a separate agreement from this. Their purchase was, the top of Birch Road, Birch Grove, Birch Walk and the Birch Road area, along with Holly Road and the land alongside the area the Johnson family later purchased.

Murder on Stanley Road

A most interesting event of this era was the unsolved murder of Frederick Walter Jeffs of 12, Stanley Road, Quinton, on Good Friday, April 19, 1957; it managed to reach the national newspapers.

SHOPKEEPER "A MAN OF MYSTERY"

MURDER VERDICT AT INQUEST

Walter Jeffs, aged 37, shopkeeper, whose battered body was found in a woodland grave on Good Friday, was a "man of mystery in his movements at night," and that probably hampered police inquiries, said the Coroner, Mr. George Billington, at the resumed inquest yesterday at Birmingham.

A verdict of murder by some person or persons unknown was returned by the jury.

Earlier, Mrs. Betty Jeffs, now living at Wilton Road, Bentley Heath, Warwickshire, said her husband agreed to a divorce a week before his death. They had been in business in Stanley Road, Quinton, but she went to live with a Mr. Kenneth Gilbert Dent.

In reply to the coroner she said that as far as she knew all stock for the shop was bought through legitimate trade channels.

STRUCK AGAIN

Dr. F. E. D. Griffiths, pathologist, said that he thought Jeffs was first struck when standing near his van. Then he had been put in the van, and at some stage he partially recovered. Bloodstains in the vehicle could have been caused through his being struck again.

Miss Sonia Winifred Weldon, of Edward Road, Quinton, said that at 11.10 p.m. on Maundy Thursday she saw a girl in the doorway of Jeffs's shop. The girl wore a dark, fitted coat and no hat, was not very tall, and young. "She drew back into the doorway again. I had reached the entry by the side of the shop when I saw a grey van turn round and come out frontways." The headlamps were put on and it stopped to pick up the girl. The van then drove off towards Hagley, but witness could not see who was driving.

PUZZLE OF VAN

Summing up, the coroner said it was fairly certain that Jeffs made some kind of an appointment with a young woman on Maundy Thursday. At 9.10 p.m. that day he was seen driving out in his van and no one saw him alive again. His poodle was seen between 10.30 p.m. and 11 p.m. alone.

A puzzling feature was that two witnesses had said they saw Jeffs's van by his shop between 10.45 p.m. and 11.10 p.m. that night. "You may wonder who was driving. Was it the murderer or was it Jeffs?" asked the Coroner.

Figure 25 The Times June 21st 1957.

Figure 26 Stanley Road 1956.

Figure 27 Jeffs sweets and tobacco shop 1956.

Figure 28 Johnson's.
On the reverse of the photograph, it says "old out door 'Johnson's 73, Birch Road 1956.

James Turner and his wife Maria (nee Johnson) were the first tenants of this outdoor. Their great grandson Peter Charles Turner has photographs which can be seen on the Quinton Local History Society web site with an interesting précis of the Turner family history. The Johnsons' who were equally as high profile, came from Ladywood and became an important family in our local history, purchasing and building houses on the site, which at one time was home to the brick workers and their families. Charles H Johnson purchased the land from the Galtons who had purchased a lot of the land in 1855. Johnson lived above it and used the shop as a provisions store with his sister Mrs Tuffley and her daughter.

After Charles death the off licence remained in the family and was taken over by F.C. Johnson in around 1937, he and his wife Maria ran out the shop turned outdoor. The Johnson name can be seen on close inspection of the sign to the left of the building. Maria ran the shop whilst her husband was establishing his basket making business on Birch Road. She died in 1978 and it looks as if this photograph was taken at the end of the tenancy before being knocked down.

Lucy Dearn remembers that Ben Johnson bought the old brickwork properties and rented the terraced houses out whilst developing the land and gardens into piggeries and an orchard. Other Johnsons', of which there were many, owned a variety of businesses and homes.

Hawthorn House, The Hawthorns, Beech Lanes

Of the many cottages and houses that once stood on Hawthorn Farm very few remain, but Hawthorn House, now 378 and 378a still stands. Hawthorn House, Hagley Road West has had a varied and interesting past, changing its facade and purpose with the passage of time. Today's Georgian appearance is very different from the facade of 100 years ago.

Figure 29 The Hawthorns House
378, 378a, Hagley Road West.

The earliest record of the plots goes back as far as the High Court of Chancery Judgement of 1856 when Ann Hill's will was contested by Stanley Millar the plaintiff v Joseph Aldridge Bond, John Southerdon Burn *and others* as defendants. Ann's will was to provide few clues as to who Millar and Bond were. Stanley Millar was left a painting of a Mr Millar, whether it was of himself or a relative is unknown but he was clearly unhappy with this decision, perhaps he was promised or hoped for land or property.

Joseph Bond bequeathed something (unknown as the documents are missing) to John Southerdon Burn who was an executor to Ann's will. When Ann's father died, he had left instructions for the farm and lands to be sold which, for some reason, they were not. As Ann had not inherited the farm in its entirety (as some part of Bristnall fields and others unnamed plots were sold off separately), lots of confusion followed and as some of the documents pertaining to the problem are missing, it is unlikely that the exact problem will ever be revealed. All that is clear is that the dispute it fell in the favour of John Owen, if he was on Millar's side or Bond's is not recorded. It does state though that The Hawthorn House was on plot number five at the auction, therefore it gives the plan of Hawthorn Farm a point of reference.

**Figure 30 The Hawthorns House.
Beech Lanes, The Griffiths family shoe factors, back warehouse.**

It had been suggested that in the early life of this house there was a coach entrance through one side of it. No one was able to confirm this and the exterior offers no clue of such an entrance. However, patience was rewarded when a clue unwittingly arrived via Andrew Maxam. He had a photograph of the Griffiths Family Shoe Factors of Beech Lanes but was unsure of the location of the premises. Having recently visited this property, it was apparent that 378 and 378a was at one time the shoe factors and the deeds of the property confirmed it. This enables us to fill in a few more gaps in the history of both the house and our local trades.

This picture (figure 30) is taken from the rear of the house and closer inspection reveals an archway in the brickwork centre left of the picture, the brickwork below it is more defined and the window is a sympathetic addition to the perspective. It is obvious now that there was indeed a coach entrance through the building which meant that the one house was considerably larger than the narrower cottage adjoining it which had a door fronting Birch Road. Today the windows have been altered but in the main, you can still see it is the same building. Intriguingly the houses share a chimney in the centre of the house. The one house has the attractive fireplace and the other holds the chimneybreast! Presumably occurring when the house was altered and the coach way was removed.

Lucy Dearn remembers it as "Griffiths, the Shoe people" as it was when this photograph was taken, she remembers her father going to Griffiths for boots as they were the sole suppliers locally, the house is clearly one property at this stage. The woman in the centre is taking a photograph of the photographer! A picture probably lost to us now. The enlargement reveals many boxes in the upstairs windows which are also held by the men who are wearing heavy looking aprons. A very small ghostly Queen Victoria styled lady can be seen between the second and third man to the right, the original picture is a little more clear but still ghostly nevertheless, it could possibly be one of the daughters unable to resist seeing the photographer at work, unless of course you know otherwise......

Allen Griffiths bought The Hawthorns House from John and Joseph Owen, the sons of John Owen, beneficiaries in Anne Hill's will. The Griffiths family used the building in its entirety as they operated their shoe business from both there and a warehouse on Birch Lane. Allen Griffiths lived there with his wife Kath, and children Ada, Isobel, Ernest, William and George, who are all listed as "workers" within the business.

Allen Griffiths died in 1919. His son Ernest Amos, and daughter Isobel sold the house off to Frederick Duggins in 1920.The house and cottage became separate properties and a transformation of the exterior took place. The Griffiths' sold the corner house in 1935 to Lancelot Lloyd, who had market stalls and sold garden furniture. Their daughter Kitty went to school with budding research assistant, Lucy Dearn, who was able to explain the sale. Then followed several changes of ownership and lessees in quick succession, one was to builder brothers William Horace Strong and Redvers Horace Strong followed by Mr Atack. Coincidentally, Mr Atack was interviewed for the chapter on the Red Lion public house, he remembers helping his brother Gilbert Atack move in to the corner house and assisted him with the renovations in 1954.

Figure 31 Lindsay and Chapman.

The land around the houses began to transform too although Lindsay and Chapman the builders Merchants which was next door, remained for a considerable while longer. The property can be just seen in figure 31 and was later demolished to build The Hawthorn flats.

By auction 1931 March 27th.

In March 1931, Mr Lancelot Lloyd puts up four lots for sale at an auction held at The Grand Hotel in Birmingham. The auction included the house in figure 30 by now known as two separate homes Hawthorn House and the adjoining Elm Tree house. The third house at auction was Hawthorn cottage that fronts Birch Lane and backed on to Hawthorn House on the corner of Holly Bush Hill and Birch Lane.

The advertisement refers to the extensive renovations of Hawthorn house, complete with: good cellarage, two heated greenhouses a range of buildings all electrically lighted throughout, a foresight combination grate and modern mantels, all at considerable cost to Mr Lloyd. The advertisement extols the virtues of the properties being placed on the widened and improved main road into the City of Birmingham.

Elm tree house is rented out to a Mr Charles Johnson, (well known in the area) who provides revenue of £52 per year and is credited for having: a white roughcast elevation, four good bedrooms a coal scullery. The rears of these two properties were also offered for sale along with valuable freehold building estate with frontages to Birch Lane as lot five.Finally lot six which was Hawthorne (sic) cottage on Birch Lane, a "nice" house presenting a 15ft wide and 170ft deep garden suitable for paultry (sic) Horticultural or business purposes.

Preliminary notice of Auction to take place in April next.

**The property of
Mr Lancelot Lloyd by Messers
Jones, son and Vernon.**

Figure 32 Smethwick telephone Saturday 21st March 1931.

GARDEN   REQUISITES
and
BUILDING MATERIALS

LINDSAY & CHAPMAN

300 HAGLEY ROAD WEST

Phone: WOO 2180

All kinds of Rustic Work a speciality

Figure 33 Lindsay and Chapman.

Figure 34 Hawthorn Croft 1955.

Figure 35 Stanley Road and Hagley Road 1955.

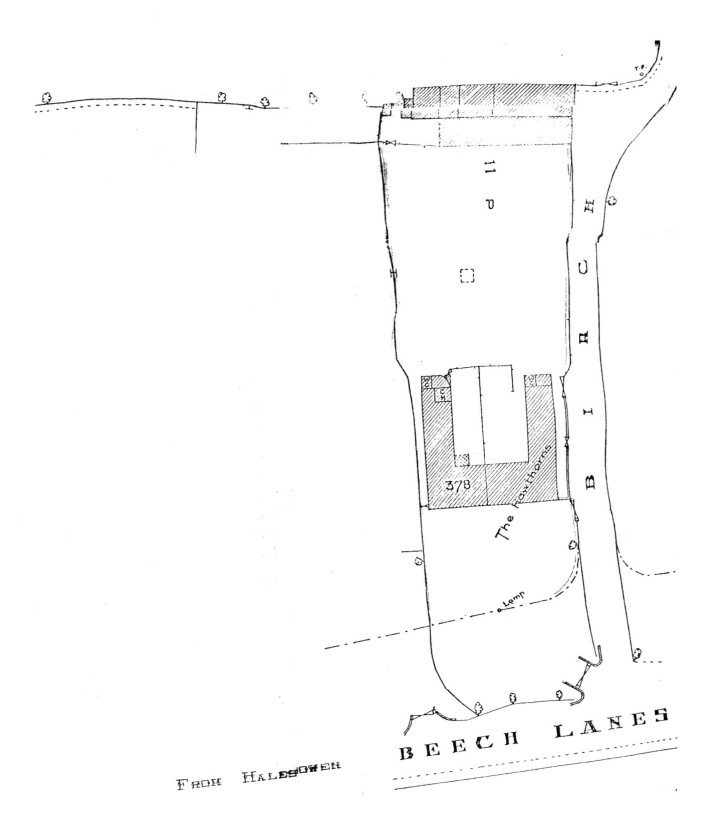

Figure 36 Plan which shows the long driveways to The Hawthorns House, Beech Lanes.

The plan indicates how long the drives were, sweeping their way up to the houses off Beech lanes. Birmingham Corporation purchased the gardens for road widening and renamed it Hagley Road West.

Lot Six
Bounded by good roads on three sides. Little Red Hill, Great Meadows. 2 acres, 2 roots, 14 poles.
To include the original Holly Bush Inn.
This became Hagley Road West, Clive Road and Holly Bush Grove area.
Aunt Polly's cottage.

Figure 37 Aunt Polly's cottage.

Aunt Polly's cottage, is a painting held in the Powell family. Dave Yates offers some notes on the Powell's background".

"Aunt Polly was a Reacord, the sister of Harry/Henry Powell's wife Phoebe. She lived with a brother, George, a bit slow in speech through crawling into a barn as a child and being kicked by a cow. Polly washed clothes for the people in 'the big houses…She took the washing back and forth in a three wheeled wicker basket, pushing it for a mile or more from where she lived near the Holly bush".

Figure 38 The Old Holly Bush Inn.

The Old Holly Bush Inn

The hill winding its way up to Bearwood was, as many of you know once called Holly Bush Hill, taking its name after the public house that stood on what is now the main Hagley Road West. Once The Hawthorns name had disappeared from that area at around the turn of the century, the hill and the name for the local area shifted to the "Holly Bush". The old Holly Bush was knocked down to accommodate the road widening and moved its premises to what was originally opened as a Hotel in May 1937. It was later called Jefferson's and more recently the Toby Carvery Quinton. Once again, it has returned to its original status of Hotel in the guise of Inn Keepers Lodge, although the "Holly bush" name is on one of its signs on the car park and there is a carved Stone Holly bush above the entrance inside from the original hotel building work.

The name also lives on in the hearts of the older generation at the Holly bush parade a name that is fast disappearing. The BP garage has a very attractive Holly Bush in the brickwork on the side of the building and the site of the old pub gardens further up the hill towards Bearwood bears the name Holly Bush Croft and The Holly Bush medical centre.

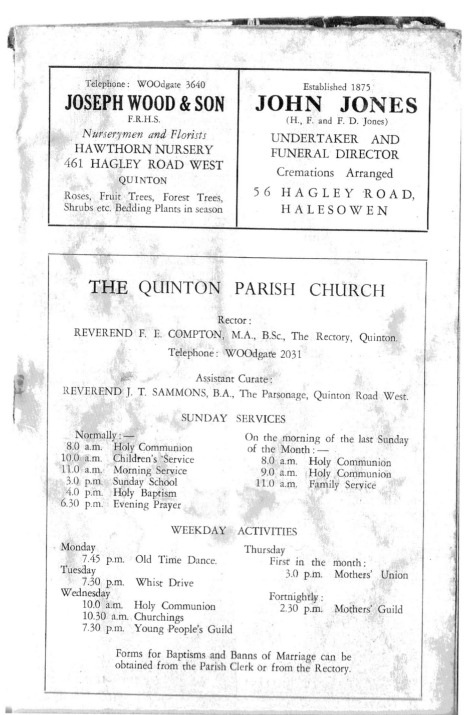

Figure 39 Hawthorn Nursery.

**Advertisement for Joseph Wood of Hawthorn Nursery,
from The Quinton Parish magazine, 1952 this nursery stood on what remained of lot 6.**

Joseph Wood's sister Emma married a Birch and they lived on Perry Hill, (more details on page 87) and Lucy Dearn informs us that Mrs 'Granny' Wood was the local midwife to Quinton, she delivered all the Dearn babies in Lucy's era.

The New Holly Bush

Smethwick Telephone Sat 30th March 1937.

An interesting article that gleans some architectural light on the new "old" Holly Bush.

Yesterday (Friday) Mitchell's and Butler's Limited opened their latest and newest house "The Holly Bush" at Quinton, which has been specially designed to supply a long felt want in refreshment houses. It not only caters for the many people who require refreshment for travelling, but special attention has been given to provide recreation and enjoyment for the local inhabitants.

This new house provides a large and modern bar panelled in oak, for men and women who require refreshment under the most hygienic conditions and surroundings. The temperature of the cellar is automatically controlled which ensures the beers being kept in perfect condition throughout the year.

The ladies and gentleman's smoke room is a particularly pleasing room, panelled in marble with the floor laid in a very modern tiled pattern design which is silent to walk on. The gentleman's smoke room has been panelled in Australian walnut, with a floor laid in a similar manner to the other smoke room. Special attention has been given to the question of service and the design has been so worked out to allow the service to control the various rooms with the utmost speed and efficiency.

A suite of rooms on the first floor is approached by a separate entrance. This suite comprises large ballroom of modern design, which has been panelled in Australian walnut and has a buffet adjoining, panelled in sycamore. The buffet has an entirely separate entrance.

The ballroom is particularly impressive which its stage and decorated ceiling which embodies an advanced system of concealed and subdued lighting effects. Leading off the ballroom are spacious cloakrooms, which have been provided for ladies and gentlemen.

The exterior of the Holly Bush has been built in a simple Georgian manner, with rough cast facing and Westmoreland green slated roof, and the main central entrance in guiting stone.

The grounds are laid out in the form of a garden, together with large terraces, a separate shelter, and pergolas. In addition, a large garden service has been provided to supply the garden with refreshments efficiently and quickly. A full size crown bowling green has also been laid out, complete with bowling pavilion This new house of Mitchell's & Butler's limited will be considered as something real in architecture, and an asset to the Quinton District. The Architects were Messrs. Batemans, 18, Bennets Hill, Birmingham.

Figure 40
The new Holly Bush standing on the edge of The Hawthorn Farm, opposite lots seven and eleven in the auction sale.

Figure 41
At the BP garage opposite the Holly Bush carvery, there is a brickwork relief of a holly leaf on the wall.

Lot Seven

The Hawthorn farmhouse, buildings and homestead. Fronting to the said Turnpike Road and several pieces or parcels of land adjoining thereto, known as ; The Honeysuckle, The barn close, The Pear tree piece and part of the House meadow. Containing 12 acres, 1 root, 0 poles or thereabouts, farmed by Mr Cooper.

By the census of 1881, the latter was farmed by Henry Nicholls and House meadow was then called Conegre Leasow.

Today, known as Hagley Road West and the Perry Hill area, Wood Green Road and the roads names after the Wood family.

These fields in lots of seven, eight and nine on the 1855 plan, appear to have been at one time attached to the fields running parallel behind them called; Near High field, Far High Field, Cow Leasow and Little Meadow, but by the purchase of 1855, they had been sold off. A plan showing the lands of a Mr Gardener in 1802 suggest that fields sold by Lyttelton of fifteen acres in the 'pear tree piece in Worcestershire' could have been the fifteen acres that the family sold off when selling to Troughton. The fact that Mr Wood took possession of and gave his name to these combined lands at a later point, supports the theory that they were adjoined.

This tranquil scene of a chocolate box village is so far removed from the traffic on the Hagley Road West Island at the Holly Bush, it becomes difficult to imagine that it is in fact the same place. It is the most important of all the 'lots' of the 1855 sale as it both places The Hawthorns geographically and contains the actual farmhouse and buildings.

Figure 42 The Hawthorn Farm painted by W. Nicholls.

This oil painting is one of two paintings, which have opened many doors creating a picture of life at the one time hamlet of The Hawthorns in the area of The Quinton.

The photographs which will appear shortly were taken at the turn of the century and are taken approximately fifty years (possibly more) after this painting was done, the changes even then are considerable. When viewed together they reveal the development of both the cottage industries and road.

Galton had purchased this lot in 1855 and quickly sold it on to the Wood family in 1856 after taking what lands he needed to adjoin to his own. Thomas Wood (1796-1870) was a wealthy chain manufacturer from Colley Gate. Wood was a man of means he could be relied upon to make generous donations to non conformist causes and was frequently called upon to attend stone laying ceremonies at local chapels of which there were once many in Lye and Cradley. He opened community events, distributed food to the poor each year around Christmas time and was frequently mentioned in the newspapers for donating and distributing tea, plum cake and butter.

He died on 15th December 1870 and is interred at the Lye Congregational Church. He left a large estate to settle; the many beneficiaries included churches and Schools in Lye, the New Connection Chapel Colley Gate, the Baptist Chapel, the Mount Zion Chapel and many more, the list is endless. The later were to receive £5.00 each and it was distributed to the poor on New Year's Day.

After Wood died, the income from The Hawthorn Farm was left to his wife Sarah along with bank shares and stock in the London and North Western Railway Company. The Hawthorn Farm estate went to his two nephews, George Swinford Wood and James Wood Aston. They too received generous shares in railway companies such as Stourbridge Railway Company, Great Western Railway Worcester Engine Company and the Cambrian Testing Company. Other shares distributed throughout the family were those in The Cradley Heath Gas Company.

In 1873 one of the nephews James Wood Aston, died. He had resided at the Elms in Cradley with his wife, who was well provided for upon his death. She continued to keep up with her late husband's charitable donations, for instance, she gave an organ at the cost of £400 in memory of her late husband to the church and a peal of eight bells costing £600, which had previously won a prize at the Vienna exhibition. The Bells were re-hung and re-bushed by Groves of Birmingham, but sadly she never heard them ring as she died in 1875 age 42, seven months before the bells were finished.

Once Mrs Wood had died, the farm became the property of George Swinford Wood a landscape artist. He lived with his brother but spent much of his time at Bodlondeb, Conway. He took an active part in the work of the Royal Cambrian Society with whom he was associated with from 1888, just a few years after the institution was established. Several of his pictures have been hung in the Royal Academy at Conway and there are several references to him in the famous art book *Allgemeines Kunstler-Lexion; Artists of the World*. Ascribed to his name are several pieces, to include, "R*epose*"", *Shut out*" and "*The dozing African*".

George Swinford and his son Thomas Henry Wood took the decision to sell off the farmland, breaking the Wood family chain, which had spanned over 40 years. They had leased most of it out and the lessees in turn sub-leased it. It remained farming land in the main until the building boom of the 1930s.The Wood's name remains in the roads, Oak, Holly Bush, Chestnut, Cedar Forest and Elm Croft.

The Cradley Bells

Hark; the Cradley Bells are ringing
Sounding sweetly down the vale
In the lofty Belfry swinging
For they float upon the gale.

Others, perhaps may sound far louder
Noisy, clanging, boisterous bells.
The thought of size may make the prouder
Not so sweet as Cradley Bells.

When along the breeze they quiver
With their notes so true and clear.
Pleased, they say across the river.
"hark, the Cradley Bells I hear".

Neighbours, too are often telling
how upon a summers day.
Cradley Bells so sweetly swelling.
May be heard for miles away.

York may boast its mighty Peter
Torn is Oxfords talk and pride
But the Cradley Bells are sweeter
Sweetest on the riverside.

Eight sweet Bells in Cradley Steeple
Wing their music through the air
Hasten hither all ye people
Hasten to the House of Prayer.

Hear us always loudly saying
Come from earthly care away
Come where all good Christians praying
Joyful keep Gods Holy day.

You on whom sane cares are pressing.
You whorl toil the week around
Come, and earn a heavenly blessing
Come, for this is holy ground.

**The Cradley Church Bells, St Peters,
written by Joseph Bissell for the re-opening of St Peters after the 1874-1875 restoration.**

Occupants of the Farmhouse

In both the census's of 1841 and 1851 The Hawthorns was farmed by The Nicholls or Nicholds family (spelling varies) for two generations, until 1856 when it went into the care of a Mr Cooper, all whilst under the ownership of Mrs Ann Hill. The Coopers were the last tenant farmers of The Hawthorns.

By the census of 1881, the farmhouse was occupied by yet another Wood family, not related to the previous owners, which is sure to confuse. John Wood lived with his wife Hannah and their ten children, Fanny, Fred, Mary Ann, Joseph, Emma, John junior, Charles, Tom, Hannah junior and Eliza, many of them continued to live and work locally. Their names appear consistently as high profile members in The Hawthorns community.

The Hawthorn Farm buildings

Figure 43 The Hawthorns.

The farm buildings to the left of this picture were the last remaining barns of Hawthorn Farm House, (see figure 3). There are more buildings than the painting by Nicholls reveals which suggests the pictures were, either taken some time later or the artist chose not to put them all in. One of these buildings became Partridge brothers the file makers, now long since gone to being replaced by Smith Brothers, Mandy Jane children's clothes, Woolworths, a video store and Masquerade Costume Hire, of which only the latter survives. When the farm buildings were demolished, a new straighter road was created into Birmingham, but taking essentially the same route.

Lucy Dearn has been an invaluable source of information and her memories are consistent. She has lived in the area all her life she remembers moving down to the Hawthorns in 1933 with her parents and sister, Lucy was born up on Holly Bush Hill in 1916. By this time the farmhouse had long gone and Lucy has no memory of it but remembers the buildings when they were the file cutters "Partridge's".

Lucy remembers that in the 1920s, the School headmaster Mr Clarke came into their classroom and told them that Beech Lanes was to be renamed and that their address was to change to 498 Hagley Road West. When the road was renamed, the cottages were demolished and the family moved up to Birch Road where Lucy and Eileen lived for 40 years or more.

The picture (figure 44) shows her mother Mrs Florence Dearn at the front of the cottage that they rented from the Partridge's at the Hawthorns.

**Figure 44 Lucy Dearn's mother, Florence
at The Hawthorns.**

Figure 45 Quinton School Photograph.

Back row:,, ? Philpot, Beryl Parry, Pearl Price, unknown Beatie Sadler, Barbara ? Dorothy Clay, Muriel Basterfield.
Middle Row: Beryl Dugmore, Annie Guest, Lily Tatton,? Pritchard, Lucy Dearn, Margaret Yeomans, Mavis Bill (both of Hagley Road).????
Front Row ? Young, ? Jones, Edie Walker, Lucy Smith, Edie Parkes.

Figure 46 Lucy's Grandfather James, Jack Yeomans and Lucy.

The picture on page 76 is Jack Yeomans with Lucy Dearn and Lucy's Grandfather James Powell in the background. The picture (figure 46) was taken in the 1920s on a stile just below where White Road is today. Lucy remembers the photograph being taken on the field beside the allotment where they stood whilst a football match was underway. The picture was taken by Jimmy Young, a butcher from Birch Road.

The Smith Brothers

Smith Bros. (Quinton) Ltd.

Smiths occupied the land on which the tranquil scene in the painting once stood. It was established in 1927, the proof of this establishment being defined by Cliff Smith (one of the founder brothers) when a sign emblazoned with the Smith Bros. (Quinton) Ltd scroll was erected by Ran Smith, above their first workshop at 570 Hagley Road West, Quinton, Birmingham. At that time, which was during the recession of the late twenties, Stan, Ran and Cliff Smith, were like so many other people at the time - looking for work, and decided to try and go it alone. They already lived in the property so had an available site.

They started with the manufacture of timber incubation units for chickens, known as "Foster Mothers". They also made sheds, greenhouses, garages, porches, verandahs and generally anything constructed in wood that people in their vicinity required. They managed to make a go of this, and being as they needed to purchase nails, screws, paint, glass, putty, etc, they decided to sell such items from 570 Hagley Road West and hence the Smith Bros, (Quinton) Ltd, Ironmongers was opened.

The row of cottages to the right of figure 47 was later acquired by Smith Brothers. However, they eventually out served their purpose and they remained uninhabited for many years although the frontages were to remain in tact albeit bricked up, probably for security purposes.

Figure 47 Smith Bros.
The cottages and Smiths Bros and were knocked down to create Guardian house.

Figure 48 Smith Bros staff.

Established 1875

JOHN JONES

(H., F. and F. D. Jones)

UNDERTAKER AND
FUNERAL DIRECTOR
Cremations Arranged

56, HAGLEY ROAD, HALESOWEN

CHIROPODY

Consult your local Chiropodist

MR. F. TOUGH
M.S.S.CH.
30 LEWIS ROAD, QUINTON
BIRMINGHAM, 32

All Foot Ailments painlessly and carefully treated Moderate fees

---

Quinton Preparatory School and Kindergarten

provides an up-to-date thorough education for boys and girls from five years of age. Pupils prepared for Secondary School Examinations. Qualified staff. Interviews arranged by letter to Principal

MISS V. WARTH, H.N.F.U.
23 Forest Rd. (off Stanley Rd.) Quinton

Telephone: WOOdgate 3640

Joseph Wood & Son
F.R.H.S.
Nurserymen and Florists

HAWTHORN NURSERY
461, HAGLEY ROAD WEST, QUINTON

Roses, Fruit Trees, Forest Trees, Shrubs etc. . . . . . Bedding Plants in season

---

THE LAWNS EVENING PREPARATORY SCHOOL

WARLEY (near Warley Odeon)

This old-established School gives Evening Preparation for all children entering for the admission Examinations to local Grammar and Technical Schools. Fully Qualified, experienced graduate tutors, and up-to-date methods have secured brilliant results in the past few years. (Ninety per cent. of our pupils gained admittance to Grammar Schools during 1948). Terms are moderate. Ideal conditions.

For appointments Phone BEA 1545.

PORTABLE BUILDINGS

GENERAL WOODWORKERS, HARDWARE STORES, RETAIL TIMBER, PAINTS GLASS ETC.

SMITH BROS. 570, HAGLEY ROAD WEST
QUINTON, BIRMINGHAM 32

Telephone: WOOdgate 2261-2

Figure 49 Advertisement for Smith Bros.
From The Quinton Parish Magazine (c1974).

Figure 50 The New Holly Bush Inn.
The (new) Holly bush and Smiths van.
You can just about make out the barrage balloon above the middle chimney
and to the left above the telephone box you can barely see what is the
direction sign to the air raid shelter.

Figure 51 Midland Red Bus to Dudley.

Figure 52 Wood Green Road 1955.

Figure 53
Rudge's fruit and
vegetable cart. Rudge's
fruit and vegetable shop
entered their horse and
carriage for a Quinton
festival in the 1930s, the
picture was taken from
the cottages at The
Hawthorns looking over
towards the new Holly
Bush Inn.

Hawthorn Garage

David Moore sold a portion of the land to Samuel Newton, who, in turn sold a smaller portion of it to William Arthur Mills, a post office servant from Great Russell Street in Birmingham and another part to Eliza Kirby from Birmingham under a separate agreement, both sales taking place on 13th October 1896.

Mr Mills kept the majority of the plot for his own personal use selling the remaining 695 square yards to Mrs Eliza Boswell. Mrs Boswell had recently acquired some money independently from her husband by way of an inheritance and wisely decided to invest it in some land. It is at this time that the six terraced houses were built, which remain today. Mr Henry Yeomans and his brother built or played a part in the building and bought some of the property off her at the point of completion.

By 1919, the remaining land belonging to David Moore either side of the terraced houses became split into larger housing plots on one side and the land to the other side had been sold to William Arthur Mills. This was to become the Hawthorn Garage.

This land had a clause written into it by David Moore that any buildings should not be less than six feet from the boundary line, presumably to create the most from the land as possible. Additionally, that if one house is built it should be to the value of at least £120, if more than one house then they should be up to the value of £100 only. This conundrum of what to build on each piece was solved and a plan was hatched between Mr Yeomans and Mrs Boswell which enabled them to build both a larger house and six smaller houses between them.

Mr Mill's piece, which eventually became his son's property, became the independent car site next to the garage, they remained so for over eighty years, and the garage was lost only recently, when Texaco sold it for housing in 2004.

Plotting the ownership through to Texaco proved difficult but working back from a previous tenant David Browning and local historian Mike Hall, the exercise was not as tedious as it could have been.

Mr Hall sold the lease on to Billy Harrington in 1932: Billy Harrington is still fondly remembered by some local folk as they enjoyed the showroom window of his car collection. This Picture shows Billy Harrington's garage and showroom where the Texaco garage once stood. The double fronted house that he once owned is clearly painted to advertise his second hand cars.

Mr Harrington leased out the double fronted house in the picture (figures 57 and 58) to various occupants and Lucy Dearn remembers that Miss Fletcher, a teacher at Castle Road School lived there when she was a girl during the 1920s. Mr Harrington moved his family in there for some years before moving them further out to the country, as the area was quickly moving from rural idyll to fast pace urbanisation, if only he could see it today!

The house was knocked down in the mid 1970s and I thank David Browning both for the use of the picture and for the foresight in taking it in the first place. Harrington held it until 1959 when he retired and sold out to Texaco.

Figure 54
Quinton Parish magazine 1954 provides another lessee for the garage (top left).

**Figure 55 The six terraced houses were commissioned by Mrs Boswell c1896.
Later purchased from the Yeomans brothers.**

Mike Hall's Grandfather, Thomas Hall leased the plot to open a garage from Eliza Kirby until 1932. Mike recalls his father referring to it, as "Hawthorn Garage" and in 1924, he described it as an iron framed garage with a corrugated iron sheet roof. It was very fortunate that Mike put pen to paper and noted his fathers memories. He said "There were 5 petrol pumps, 2 Pratts at 11d a gallon, 1 shell, 1 national Benzol at 1s 1d and one for Russian oil products at 9d a gallon".

If you are unacquainted with Francis Brett Young, 1884-1954, novelist, short-story writer, and poet, born in Halesowen, then perhaps this is an opportune moment to introduce you to him. Young wrote tranquil novels. This style could be described as pedestrian and long-winded at times but he manages to muster up enough interest through its charm and sentimentality to carry the reader to the more exciting parts. At the end of Second World War Brett Young moved to South Africa, dying in Cape Town in 1954. His ashes were returned to England and are in Worcester Cathedral.

The appearance of Tilton (Quinton) appears in *Mr & Mrs Pennington*, published in 1931.This novel is the story of two newlyweds Susan Lorimer and Dick Pennington during their first year of marriage, after a short whirlwind courtship of two weeks. They begin married life in a bungalow in Ada Road, at Tilton (Quinton), reflecting the new housing that expanded Quinton at the time, Tilton was a growing suburb of North Bromwich (Birmingham). Living in Halesowen, Quinton would have been familiar to Brett Young as he passed through it on his way into Birmingham, observing the

Figure 56 West side service station.

way of life for its inhabitants and the buildings that he describes, from the picturesque to the less attractive sights.

In this book he describes a garage in the village of "Tilton" which we know to be Quinton. It is almost safe to say that this is the very garage he is describing, as it was the only garage in Quinton to be ironed framed, all the others were brick built,

> "Until now the sleepy streets of Tilton echoed continually with the grinding of gear-pinions and the stutter of exploding petrol and its ancient buildings with their air of formal grace had become encrusted (as it were) in reticulations of staring new brick, a red and rodent ulcer eating its way into the soft green tissue on either side of a broad arterial road where a series of Jerry built shops and petrol stations concrete cinema a galvanised iron estate office and a showroom exhibiting appliances for the use if municipal gas and electricity ,had made Tilton, that shy individual hamlet, no different from hundreds of other debauched villages on the outskirts of a midland town" (179).

David and his father Walter Browning leased the garage from Texaco from 1960 to 1977 making many changes to the façade of the building giving it a more up to the minute 70s appeal.

The garage was known as West Side Garage Quinton, although when the boundaries changed the area became Oldbury. It is unlikely that Texaco's decision to retain the Quinton address was done for nostalgic purposes but for the purpose of geography, as so often deliveries for Oldbury went further north and continue to today, but with the advent of satellite navigation this is a less frequent occurrence.

Figure 57
The West Side Garage facing up the hill, with Mr Harrington's double fronted house.

As the Browning's lease approached the end of its time with only one year remaining Texaco decided to close the doors and the Browning's were left without a business in spite of having paid six months in advance for the lease. Texaco pondered on the future of the garage and site and reopened it after it was closed for a year. This time it had new tenants, as the Browning's had moved on to pastures new.

Figure 58
The Texaco garage during the Browning's lease, selling Regent petrol.

Figure 59 Walter and David Browning c1966.

Figure 60 Browning's car sales, next door to the garage.

Lot Eight

Little Leys and Part of House Meadow, which became Sunny Bank Road and part of Wood Green. Sunny Bank Road being the dividing field line of Little Leys and Part of house meadow.

Hubert Barclay Galton purchased this plot along with plots one two and three, but sold this particular one off very quickly to Thomas Wood on 25th October 1856. Wood's nephews George Swinford Wood and Thomas Henry Wood leased it out to John Darby on 25th July 1891, who in turn sub leased it to John Hodgetts Smith and Walter Leopold Smith.

The land was continuously whittled down into smaller plots at this point, therefore, too many names, loans, mortgages, leases and sub leases to be of any possible interest to the reader. However, names vital to history of the local area or names of particular interest have been observed.

John H Smith died on the 2nd April 1897 and Walter Smith died on the 9th Sept 1898 with Mary Smith as sole benefactor. Whilst in their hands the Smiths' had restrictions placed on the land to prevent a trade or business to be carried out that should cause the said J.H Smith or W.L. Smith any nuisance or annoyance to them. The brothers must have lived on the land and leased part of it out wanting the minimum of inconvenience to themselves. This land lay along the Hagley Road West and was in later years owned by the Pratt family where they ran a successful business.

John Darby of Howley Grange Farm Quinton Worcestershire and his wife Martha bought the lease for £1,300, plus interest on 14th April 1891 in the hope of building dwellings on the site. Their daughter Eliza married William Partridge. When her parents died, they left J.A Sidaway and William Partridge as benefactors in their will. They, in turn, on the 18th September 1919 sold the right to Thomas Baggs to have access over the road 10 yards wide and over the road 5 yard wide leading to a garden allotment: part of this particular plot became Sunny Bank Road. These names; Sidaway, Partridge and Darby are pertinent as they are names retained in the Quinton area today.

David Moore a nail master from Stourbridge purchased a smaller portion of the land and subsequently leased a proportion of it to Henry Yeomans, a General Dealer. The Yeomans family were locals and in the Church records and census returns they are listed as living in Quinton and Wyrlie Wiggie (Warley Wigorn), scribing as they spoke. Joseph and Harriet Yeomans had three sons William, Henry, Thomas and a daughter, Dora Alice on the census of 1881. In 1881, Joseph Yeomans was either fined 2/6d or 7 days imprisonment in 1880 for drinking after hours in the Red Lion Public house.The records in the Halesowen record do not divulge which punishment he chose.

Henry, the son of Joseph and Harriet, was listed as a crate maker in 1881 and it was he and his brother that later developed their property development skills.

Henry married Mary Jane. The couple had a daughter, Margaret whose picture was taken with Lucy Dearn, at Quinton School. Henry Yeomans built the houses close to The Hawthorn Garage; he was also recorded as a gardener, grocer, painter, and farmer to name but a few, the entrepreneur of The Hawthorns! He had so many occupations it would be safe to assume he dabbled at anything that was convenient, necessary, or lucrative at the time. Mr Yeomans lived in Quinton with one of his brothers and his family until his death in 1947, having had his allotment vegetable patch where a car park now stands selling vegetables to the locals and passers by. He also had sitting tenants in his front room and his home brewed ale to boost his income. After the domestic tenants moved out, he decided to rent out the room as a shop to a Miss Cooper where the locals collected their rations.

My former mother in law, Gladys wrote this c1989 when I asked her to recall some of her memories.

"My mother, father and two sisters, Joyce and Irene came to live in Quinton in 1933. We had been visiting Quinton for sometime watching our house 574, Hagley Road West being built. We watched it grow from the foundations to the roof and then for a long time after waiting for it to dry out, something that is no longer done. We opened the premises as green grocer store, as this was the trade my mother had run in Birmingham, my father had his own transport business 'Witcomb's'. We rented a house on Worlds End Lane for a while, then moved into the shop. "Sometime during the war my Father was approached by Mr Yeomans whom we had all known since our first arrival to Quinton, we sold his garden produce in our shop, very often having to gather it ourselves. Mr Yeomans approached my father asking him if he would be interested in buying the house as he was getting on in years and he wished to make provision for his daughter and his brother. My father agreed, the arrangement was not broadcast. Mr Yeomans would come to my father whenever he needed money, to the sum of £100 at a time; this was done with the bond being sealed at the solicitor's office.

In 1949, the shop was run as a grocers and a cafe rented off Yeomans by Miss Cooper who was there when we came to live at Quinton, her hey day was during the War when R.R soldiers were stationed across the road where the garage is now. Mr Yeomans died in 1947 but he had secretly mortgaged the house to an electrician, there was a lot of trouble over that! We got the house but Dad had to find the full market price.

The health people closed her down as the place was so dirty. My father gave her £200 to leave although he was not forced to do, Mom and Dad then burnt every thing in the shop, the counter, and all. Jack and I bought the house on 31 March 1959 after my father died at the early age of 59", (see figure 56 with the grocery van).

Mr Yeomans had indeed secretly mortgaged the house, not once but twice to a Mr Denys Edwards, an electrician on the Hagley Road and a Mr G. Norris a fish monger from Ward End. The problem became a long public legal wrangle causing ill feeling and difficulties. Mr Yeomans died on 17th March 1947 and left his solicitors to solve the problem. The solicitors could find no trace of such a transactions and it was only when Mr Norris was offered the sum of £1,947, that the claim was dropped.

Once the sale was complete Mr and Mrs Witcomb moved in, paying off Miss Cooper £200 for a speedy exit. The Public Health Department then came for a visit as it was by this time offering refreshments to local or passing trade. The Health Department was unhappy with the fact that Miss Cooper had no running water and was furnished with only a pitcher a bowl and a foul wooden counter. It concluded that the necessary alterations were made and Winnie Witcomb found herself running the shop whilst William ran his furniture business from there. The shop developed into a friendly place to pop into have a cup of tea, have a natter and collect the day's provisions. It also thrived during the war as The Royal Engineers were stationed across the road where the B.P garage is today (lot eleven) and the locals collected their rations from there. Mr Witcomb's empire of haulier, green grocer and café owner came to an abrupt end when he died suddenly in the garden of the property aged 59. The establishment was then run for many years by Gladys and Jack Creed followed by their son and his wife Kate where their two daughters Natasha and Harriet were born; becoming the fourth generation in direct line of descent to live in the house.

Miss Cooper can be seen with neighbour Miss Kesterton (fig 62) who lived with her sister and parents in the house to the left of this picture, she moved in later life to one of Yeomans houses until well into her eighties. She kept her self occupied to the end by making peg bags for everyone and gave me one as a moving in present when I first came to Quinton. She made and dressed dolls for the children of the area and enjoyed standing at the gate waiting for some responsive folk to pass by and chat.

Figure 61 Miss Longley's ration book.
This ration book dated 8th July 1940 belonged to Winifred Longley of 608, Hagley Road West, Quinton. It clearly states Miss Coopers as the retailer.

Figure 62 Witcomb's furniture removals.
Outside the shop just as Mr and Mrs Witcomb took over, here is Miss Cooper with Miss Kesterton and her dog.

Lot Nine

A very valuable piece of Land Possessing a double frontage, called Top Meadow, containing 2 acres, 3 roots, 18 poles or thereabouts.

Perry Hill lane and the Mitchell's & Butler's homes.

Pear Tree Piece was the local name used prior to its division in 1855, Perry Hill took its name from the "Perry" drink that was once made on the hill from the local fruit. The adjoining field was described as "Top Meadow, a valuable piece of land possessing a double frontage, 2 acres, 3 roots and 18 poles" in 1855. In the 1921 edition of Kelly's directories, Perry Hill is entered as "The Hawthorns Quinton from Perry Hill to Bleak House".

You can see on the photograph (figure 66) what is meant by the "double frontage" as the land could be accessed either along the Turnpike Road to the front and up Perry Hill along the side. By 1870 it was referred to as "Nursery Ground on Perry hill" and again in 1893 when Mitchell's & Butler's began purchasing plots of land along there. However, it was to be several years before the building programme went ahead. Their old minute books refer to the land having been "purchased to enhance the life of retired publicans and employees" and that "suitable land in the country had been found and purchased in Quinton". In 1909 Mitchell's & Butler's began building on Perry Hill Lane: they were called the Albert Butler memorial homes and each of the earlier houses built in 1909 and later in 1912 houses bear inscriptions. Further houses were later added on in memory of other members of the Butler family.

This incredible view of the hill taken shows that the houses have crept up along the north side of the hill, but have yet to be developed on the south side. The horse that can be seen centre right of the picture could have been a Mitchell's & Butler's dray horse as they and others used the land for grazing their horses. Mitchell's & Butler's had built some of their houses at this point but they are out of view.

Figure 63 Perry fields.
Real photo card of area, Quinton, pre-Quinton Expressway.
Card gone through post in 1944, but the picture dates back to around 1934.

There are piles of bricks in the fore ground, which could be for several reasons: building new Mitchell's & Butler's houses, building preparations for the electricity sub station or the demolition of some of the older house that stood nearby at the time.

This later view was from the site opposite an old large old house with columns either side of the front with attractive foliage and trees to protect which partially hid the house. Rumour has it the original house burnt down and the owners were so upset that they had it built exactly the same way. There is a large house on that site now, which has unusual chimney features and part of the current front wall is from a previous building, it could be the re built house.

This land had countless streams running through it and the piece of green to the right of this picture which is frequently referred to locally as the "green triangle" collected all the rain water and holds the drainage. Hence this marshy slough, which is noted on many old maps. It still serves that purpose today along with a place to house the sub station and provides a nice green plot to walk the dog.

Figure 64 Perry Hill c1950.

Figure 65 Perry Hill facing West.

Figure 66 Perry Hill fields.

The Mitchell's & Butler's houses

Figure 67 The Alms houses.
Perry Hill lane c1930, the two houses far right were built in 1909
and two further houses added in 1912.

**Figure 68 Mitchell's & Butler's Alms house, with attractive memorial plaque.
The plaque on the 1909 houses reads "Erected to the tenants and employees of Mitchell's and Butler's, to the memory of a great friend".**

In 1905, it was the Steeples family that nurtured the land, Mr John Steeples; the nurseryman lived there on Perry Hill with his wife Matilda, two daughters and his son Charles who was the plant salesman. The land had not changed much over the years and it was listed as being nursery land to a company called Hunter and Co, as was much of the farm land at one point. They were a well-established seeds company having a warehouse in Hockley, from there they packaged and post-ed out their seeds. They leased the plots seven, eight and nine through Lyttelton's, the Troughton's and the Hill's ownership until they ceased trading in 1828.

The corner plot on Perry Hill and Perry Hill Lane was the last field to be built on, hanging on to its nursery status for as long as possible with the help of Mr Keates a retired police officer that kept a piece of land close to his house there. Betty Rose of Elm Croft says she remembers him enjoying chatting to everyone that went past as he held the plot for the company of the passers buy as much as his gardening. A stream ran through the field and neighbours report that there was also a pond, which Mitchell's & Butler's used for the horses next to an allotment area.

The building boom of the 1930s

Mitchell's & Butler's were the first to build on Perry hill lane due to the health giving benefits of the countryside, it was many years before the complete transformation from countryside idyll to urbanisation was complete.

The main building schemes began in the 1930s with several builders purchasing local plots with a view to building houses. Godfrey Lewis builders built on Perry Hill and also locally along with Dares whose 'Dares to build' mantra was a popular sight. Yates the builders, with Yeomans building a few privately further round the corner. Bass records show that in 1950 Mitchell's & Butler's purchased 5,500 square yards of freehold land for £3,437 on the hill off Mrs Emma Birch. Mrs Birch owned one of the few large abodes on the hill. Mrs Irene Moulding (now sadly deceased) was related to the Birch family through her Aunt Emma, nee Wood who married Thomas Birch, they lived on Perry hill in a large house between Lewis Road and the Wolverhampton Road, probably Warley House as a Philip Henry Birch is in residence there in 1927 and a Mary Birch in 1951.

BIRCH FARM

ESTATE QUINTON

CORNER OF PERRY HILL & HAGLEY RD WEST

YOUR ATTENTION IS CALLED TO: -

A limited number of separate lounge and dining room type houses now in the course of erection.

The design is particularly pleasing

Comprising

Price £395

Total Deposit £20

No Legal road charges

Weekly 16/6 clear

Large lounge with bay window,

Dining room, Tiled kitchen with Quarried floor and fitted cabinet.

Three good sized bedrooms (Bay window to front bedroom)

tiled bathroom and panel bath, lavatory basin and

wc. patent storm proof windows.

Garage Accommodation.

Figure 69 Smethwick Telephone 6th Jan 1934.

This advertisement was featured in the Smethwick Telephone on Jan 6th 1934 and again in January 18th 1936. Later on that year the same advertisement was to appear with a partnership between Godfrey Lewis and company at the revised price of £375 and 16/6d clear and "Birch Farm Estate" was born, a name that is lost to us now. Birch Farm Estate once with entitled Pear Tree Piece and Top Meadow, which is now Perry Hill Lane and Perry Hill, Warley.

Figure 70 The Birch Farm estate advertisement.

Mr Yates built the two houses on Quinton Hill to the left of Yeomans properties, but clearly not in competition with them. They survive today as fine, solid, semi detached properties. He lived in one for a while before selling it on to The Kesterton and Williams families, names that were synonymous to the Hawthorns area for many years. Yates then built himself a new house between Clive Road and the Holly bush, he also had one at the back on Sunny Bank Road, a true Quintonian as he didn't move very far away.

Quinton improvement scheme

Early in the New Year there will be commenced on the main road at Quinton
one of the most important public improvement schemes in the annals
of this vastly changed area.

The particular centre of the scheme is on the old turnpike road, now forming a singular
promontory amid all the change and widening projects that have been carried out by City and
by private enterprise. Many will be anxious to see the old buildings before they are removed
and may be someone will be inspired to write something of their history, for they have played
as large part in the life of an ancient parish.

We understand that in connection with the development to be undertaken,
there is to be erected an imposing building for a branch of the
Birmingham Municipal Bank.

It will be at the corner of college road. Mr J.A Swan who designed the cemetery
chapel at Quinton, and who has been Highly commended for so worthy
interpreting the wishes of the city authorities, and indeed,
of all who appreciate the quiet and reposeful character of the buildings
within Gods acre, has been given the commission for
this important work.

Mr Swan has carried through many interesting schemes including the
Mander memorial at Saint Peters Church Wolverhampton, the designs for
which were exhibited at the Royal Academy in 1932.

Figure 71 Newspaper report.

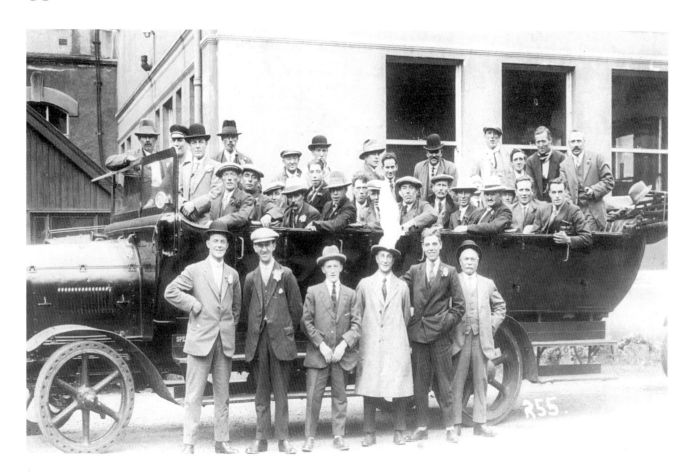

Figure 72 Yates the builders, works outing.

Back row: left to right William Dearn (Bill's father) who lived in one of Yeomans houses.
4th on the left Frank Dearn, Lucy Dearn's uncle.
Middle row 2nd on the left John Dearn Lucy's Father.
Front Row: Man in the light Macintosh was Mr Yates himself.

The privileged of Perry Hill

The Brennand's were a wealthy family owning several public houses in Smethwick; they had servants in the large house initially with a carriage and pair (of horses) and later a car with a chauffeur to take them to church on Sundays, they have retained their name locally in Brennand Road. Tony Rosser's Book "Quinton Around and About" has more information about the Brennand family.

Another family living on the Hill in 1881 were the Brecknells'; George Brecknell was a Jeweller and lived with his wife Lavinia, his five sons and one daughter also called Lavinia. It been rather difficult to ascertain which house they lived in but most people living on Perry Hill were families of means, there are no nail makers mentioned here!

There are six entries in the 1921 Kelly's directory on Perry Hill at the Hawthorns;

Mrs Sarah Elizabeth Norton, Philip Henry Birch, Frederick William Naylor at Warley House William Brennand at Perry Hill. Mrs Mary Brinton at the Dairy William, Henry Cooper Farmer at Warley Farm, locally known as Cooper's Farm.

In 1927, there are some additions: W.H Jones at Oakfields, possibly at the site around Oak Road. Mr Philip Henry Birch, Mrs Henrietta Nightingale and Mr Arthur Hackett farm bailiff to Mrs Nightingale. This last property could be the house known as High Tors or High Tor, which stood opposite Forest Road possibly built by the Nightingale family that owned Langley Forge. It was used as a home guard base during the war and also a private college. It is now the site of four town houses at around 50, Perry Hill Road. By 1851 Mrs Mary Birch, resides at Warley House Perry Hill.

An interesting snippet from the past on Perry Hill at Worcester record office in the Court Register, reads as follows:

"Tucker George, Feb 16th 1886 Of Perry Hill House, Painter. Complaint by Samuel Rowe of Beech Lanes Quinton. George Tucker went on strike yet earned 11/1d per week. He was ordered to pay 5/ 6d and costs"

The last family to be mentioned near the hill are the Smiths of Quinton mentioned earlier. They owned a large house, which has now also been demolished and stood on what is now Perry court. The large house had a warehouse at the back and beyond that a field. It was on this field that friends and neighbours remember helping to organise the horses owned by Mr Williamson for the annual donkey derby held in this field. They remember all the local children were invited to what is fondly remembered as a wonderful annual event for many years, (see figure 79).

Figure 73 A lonely goat on a hill (Perry Hill) c1956.

Lot Ten

An excellent field of Old Turf Land.

Called the GREAT HILL, situated on the rising Ground leading up to the Quinton, on the said Turnpike Road, containing 7 acres, 1 root, 30 poles or thereabouts. This land was sold in 1855 to Windmill Farm and Ivy House Farm; it eventually became Hagley Road West, part of Wilmington and Clydesdale Roads and Conway Avenue.

**Figure 74 Red Lion Hill
Quinton.
The pub is visible on the right of the bend.**

Referred to as Red Lion Hill Quinton, this was probably an error as it was often referred to locally as Red Lion Hill because of the Public House although, it was never officially called that. The original post card has a postmark of 1906, although the photograph could have been taken earlier. It was posted to Mr Horace Bragg at 13 Love Lane and reads:

"I am sending you this card, you must keep them all, with love from Aunt Lucy".

It seems Aunt Lucy was aware of the changes taking place and urged Horace to keep the cards as a record.

This lot became part of Windmill Farm after the sale in 1855 and subsequently part of the Hagley Road West, Edenhall Road, Wilmington Road and Clydesdale Road. This destroyed the rural footpath that once led from the field at the bottom of the hill, which now houses the B.P garage, the gulleys behind Conway Avenue being the last vestiges of the footpath.

Figure 75 The bus has replaced the coach and the pub has dissolved into the dual carriageway.

Quinton Hill, Quinton

Figure 76 Quinton Hill, looking up towards the church.

Figure 77 The Red Lion public house 1937, the pub sign removed in preparation for demolition.

The footpath can be seen on the old plans and there are references to an application to change its course slightly when the houses were built. The "Great Hill" of 1855 is still as "Great" today but few of us would find the time to walk it as it is an unpleasant battle against the roar of the traffic and an unhealthy attack on the lungs, it is a far easier journey to drive it or catch the bus.

The Red Lion public House once stood half way down the hill from the Church towards Birmingham, on what is now the central reservation. The road has had many titles over the years, Red Lion Hill, Lion Hill, Quinton Hill, The Turnpike Road and of course more latterly the main Hagley Road West.

Road widening scheme

The council agreed to contribute an estimate sum of £5,675 towards a £51,000 scheme for widening the Halesowen –Birmingham Road between Beech Lanes at the junction of the Birmingham Wolverhampton Rd. The proposed scheme by Birmingham provides for the addition of a second carriageway for the whole of the section maintained by Birmingham, together with a portion of the length maintained by Worcestershire from Quinton Church to the Red Lion, embracing a new roundabout of extensive dimensions at the junction of the Birmingham Wolverhampton Rd.

Figure 78 Saturday May 9th 1936 The Midland Advertiser and Wednesbury Borough News.

Figure 79 Mr Williamson with one of his horses.

In an attempt to uncover some details of the Old Red Lion public house, it became evident of just how much has been destroyed. In approaching, Worcestershire, Birmingham and Sandwell councils and receiving helpful responses, no one could find any records. Therefore, on the under-standing that there maybe very little more I could do, ironically the church was the next port of call, in the vein hope of some parishioners registering their abode as the pub. There are so few refer-ences to the Red Lion that each and every tiny piece of the jigsaw gleaned was an important one and helps to create a picture of life on 'The Hill'. So little was found that to even call them 'tiny pieces' seems an exaggeration. However, it all helps and Christ church The Quinton presented a birth and a death and the Brewery records of Bass kindly gave me the last barrelage records, hence the title of this work.

There appears to be no reference as to when it was built and as it was a rather drab uninspir-ing building, it is hardly surprising that it was not considered worthy of any note. The Red Lion or The Lion (as it was occasionally recorded as) appears on maps as far back as 1840 and offered no historical value architecturally or as a land mark. It was important in its day and however little we know about it, it is worthy of a mention before it is lost completely. As boring and as drab as it was it did fill a purpose, it served its community and provided solace and company for those that needed it. A sawdust floor, a friendly face and a jug of ale may be all that was available after a day toiling in the fields or sweating away in the heat of the nailers forge.

This first picture (figure 74) with the horse and carriage is a fascinating glimpse into life on the hill around the turn of the century. Closer inspection reveals the Hudson's soap advert on the car-riage and the soft verge that pulls in where the carriage would collect its passengers on their way into Birmingham. The public house had a clearly defined garden fence and the buildings to the right are the cottages on the plan from Trevanie Avenue deeds, which appear quite isolated.

Figure 80 Hagley Road West, note the traffic cut out opposite Perry Hill Lane, refer to figure 82.

Figure 81
The road prepares for the traffic coming from the new motorway and expressway.

Figure 82 Hagley Road West by Perry Hill lane, the cut out no longer exists.

A chronological account
of the times in the life of the Red Lion –
taken from police records, brewery records,
church records and newspapers.

James Cooper is listed in the Census of 1841 and in the Kelly's directory of that year as an industrious butcher, farmer and Licensee of the Red Lion. His servants were George Hall, Alice Green and George Blundell. Cooper's land comprised twenty acres, which he leased from yet another local family, the Bissell's whose name is given to Bissell Street. Cooper paid tythe payments to the vicar of Halesowen and Lord Lyttelton but sub leased some of the land to Joseph Harris. This plot was later used for allotments. Cooper was still there in the census of 1851 with his wife Letitia, servants John Blick from Northfield and Jane Hall from Ridgacre. By 1855, the property was occupied by the Bissell's and the map indicates a Miss Bissell as resident on it. Cooper was at the time elected Peoples Warden at Christ Church, The Quinton.

Park Hall near Kidderminster

July 31 1846

Sir

Warley Wigorn Apportionment Expenses Rate

I take leave to inform you that in order to wind up this matter I have appointed the 3rd day of August next at James Coopers the sign of the Red Lion at Warley Wigorn to receive the arrears of this rate yet outstanding when I hope you will not fail to pay the sum of £7.1.10 assessed (t)on you.

It is necessary that the rate should be collected without further delay and if not paid at the time and place above mentioned, the payment must be enforced which I should much regret.

am sir

Your very obedient servant

J Mathews

Valuers charges   £4.13. 6

Law Charges   £2. 8 4

Total   £7. 1. 10

Mr H Galton Esq.

Figure 83 Apportionment expenses collected at The Red Lion.

In 1862, a man died during a fight at one of Quinton's many pubs, The Reverend C. H. Oldfield wrote a strong letter to all the local publicans about the matter. It pointed out the ungodliness and misery associated with their trade.

"if you allow evil to be nourished under your own roof, by means of which you draw a profit, are you free from guilt? Are you innocent if, instead of doing what you can to cure the miseries of others you add to them?" (Rosser 1999.117).

It was to be a good while before relations improved between the church and the publicans in the area and there is no indication that the letter ever did any good anyway but in 1931 things took a step in the right direction as will be revealed at a later juncture.

In 1872 Records indicate that an application for an Ale House transfer From Mathew Harris to Henry Bricknell at The Old Red Lion at Quinton Hill. The petty session's book for Halesowen confirms it was granted on 20th February 1872.

In 1887

The Weekly News

Drunk and disorderly, Benjamin Preedy, a bricklayer of Quinton was charged with being drunk and disorderly on September 24th. P.C. Williams stated that he saw the defendant very drunk near the Red Lion Public House, Quinton, he also used bad language, he was creating a disturbance. The defendant having previously been convicted was fined £10 shillings and costs.

Figure 84 The Weekly News 1887.

There was a Benjamin Preedy living at lower Quinton with his wife Jemma and their five sons, perhaps he had to take them all to the pub one by one to give them "Quality time".

Brett Young demonstrates an empathy with the locals in *They Seek a Country,*

"Two Ale houses in the village brewed a turbid fluid from spoiled barley malt, but little of it was sold, Labourers had no money to spend on beer, as drink they must since only in drink could life seem bearable, they distilled in their homes a variety of fiery liquors fermenting from hogwash of crushed turnips and potato peelings and sprouting grain which stupefied at the best and at the worst made men fighting mad" (pp 51-52).

12th June 1880

Joseph Yeomans was fined for drinking after time in the Red Lion Quinton,

A two shilling and sixpence fine or 7 days imprisonment.

Figure 85 The Weekly News 12th June 1880.

The census of 1881 reveals that Emma Cheshire was the licensee residing at the Red Lion Hill. It was unclear as to whether she owned it or ran it for someone else and it was the brewery record at Bass, proved she did in fact own it. She lived there with her three daughters Emma, Mary and Clara all born in Quinton and they had two servants, Mary Barton, a domestic servant from Winchcomb in Gloucestershire and John. T. Marshall the Inn servant from Rowley Regis, John was only 15 at the time and yet no doubt he would have pulled a few pints.

Emma Cheshire, (possibly of the Cheshire family from Windmill lane Brewery) owned the pub until she retired in 1909 aged 65, having served the community for at least 28 years. During her years at the Red Lion, Emma saw her daughter Clara marry Benjamin Earl Pewtress on 18th February 1895, Benjamin's father owned the plot of land immediately opposite the public house. Clara and Benjamin had their first-born at the Red Lion and he too was named Benjamin but sadly, he died after living for only 15 minutes. Fortunately they were to go on and have more children with Cyril and Victoria Hilda born in 1902.

The Pewtress family came from Iping in Sussex and the family Christian name of Benjamin goes back for generations. Mr Pewtress later sold the land to Mr Yates the local builder who developed much of the land around Perry Hill area; he lived in one of them before selling it to the Kesterton family and moved to his new house on Sunnybank Avenue.

Police constable Henry Raybold was nicely busy for such a small village as the petty session's book for Halesowen indicates. A few of the interesting ones concerning the pub or locale vicinity are;

James Cooper, Ale house open during prohibited hours in 1884 fined, 8 shillings and costs.

Furious driving by Felix Payne.

Permitting drunkenness.

Harbouring reputed prostitutes (Joseph Smith 1883).

James Cooper. A Highway offence - fined 5 shillings and costs of 8 shillings.

James Cooper "for allowing the house to stray", this one is interesting because by this time Emma Cheshire had purchased the Red Lion so it could have been at another public house or perhaps he ran it for her.

Jesse Hadley drunk in charge of Horse and Wagon 10shillings or 7 shillings and 14 days.

On the 1st June 1843, the court sessions reveal an event, which was recorded, in the local paper of the attempted rape of Hannah Hall. The sentence was an imprisonment of two months.

Public Office Hales Owen Salop
Thursday 1st day of June 1843

On a Charge preferred by Thomas Hall on
behalf of Hannah Hall his Daughter
against

William Knight

For an Assault with intent to commit
a Rape.

Depositions of Witnesses

Hannah Hall (aged 14 years) on her oath deposeth and saith - For the last two years I have been in the Service of Mr Henry Nicholls of the Hawthorn Farm in the Parish of Hales Owen in the County of Salop and the Prisoner William Knight is Waggoner for Mr Nicholls he came there last Michaelmas - Between one and two oClock yesterday afternoon my Master sent me into his one of his fields to pick Squitch and the Prisoner was carting Manure into the same field - The Prisoner took me and shewed me where I was to begin and as I was stooping to pick the Squitch I heard somebody coming up behind me and on my looking back the Prisoner caught hold of me and tried to take liberties with me - He put his hands and attempted to pull my Clothes up and wrestled with me I resisted him and told him there was a man coming and that if he was not quiet I would hoot - The Prisoner said he didnt care and became more violent and struggled with me and threw me down on my face and afterward turned me upon my Back - He then pulled up my Clothes as far as he could and exposed my Person - I hooted Murder several times and struggled to get away but the Prisoner lay himself on me and kept me down by force and said "Damn you I'll feel you before I leave you" and attempted to force my legs apart and was unbuttoning his Trousers when my Father

came up and released me from him - After the Prisoner threw me down I hooted as loud as I was able - I was much exhausted from my struggling with the Prisoner and my Forehead was bruised and swollen from the Fall - I cried out Murder several times - There was no other Person working in the Field -

Taken and Sworn before me one of Her
Majestys Justices of the Peace for the said
County of Salop this 1st day of June 1843

The Mark of
✕
Hannah Hall

Tho⁺ Meredith

Figure 86 Deposition 1843.

Thomas Hall,   Labourer, on his oath deposeth and saith - The Witness Hannah Hall is my Daughter and is nearly 14 years old - I was yesterday employed in getting Gravel for the Roads near the field of Mr Nicholls where my Daughter was at Work - I was returning from my Dinner about Two oClock in the afternoon when I heard the Cries of "Murder 'Murder" several times - I went to the Field and there saw my Daughter lying on the ground struggling to get away from the Prisoner who was lying across her Body - As soon as I got up to them I struck the Prisoner with my Fist and knocked him off my Daughter and released her - My Daughter's Clothes were turned up and half her Person exposed The Prisoner did not see me until after I struck him he was lying across my Daughter and kept her down by main force and with his Right hand was attempting to separate her Legs which were crossed - My Daughter was crying and was much exhausted from the violence of the Prisoners Conduct Her Bonnet was crushed and her Hair hanging about her Face -   After I struck the Prisoner on the side of his Head he bled a good deal and lay on the Ground for two or three minutes -   When he got up I said to him "You "Villain I'll punish you, I'll have the Law of you

"for this" - And the Prisoner replied "You have punished me "already, you've took the Law into your own hands" - I then took my Daughter to Hales Owen and obtained a Warrant against the Prisoner and gave it to Benjamin Hill the Constable - I was about 100 yards distant when I first heard my Daughter hoot Murder.

Taken and Sworn before   The Mark of
me   X
        Tho⁵ Meredith   Thomas Hall

Benjamin Hill on his oath deposeth and saith I am a Parochial Constable for Ridgacre in the Parish of Hales Owen and apprehended the Prisoner on this Charge - I accused him of assaulting Hannah Hall and he did not deny the Charge but told me he should have loosed her if her Father had not come up - As I was bringing him to the Lockup at Hales Owen the Prisoner asked if I thought Thomas Hall would be willing to make it up and said he would give him a Sovereign to do so and asked me to make Hall that offer for him.   The Place where the Assault took place is about 400 yards from the Turnpike Road and almost as far from any House.

Taken and Sworn before
me   Benjamin Hill
        Tho⁵ Meredith

Figure 86 Deposition 1843.

It was not until 1909 that Kelly's directories give The Red Lion a street number, having previously been recorded as The Red Lion at Warley Wigorn or The Quinton, it was then given the address of 645 Red Lion Hill, Quinton.

The public house sign was used as a means of identification, which could be addressed by everyone, even the illiterate. The Old (later dropped) Red Lion Warley / Quinton featured the insignia as that of the Warley County Borough Coat of Arms which would have been a clear indication for those travelling from Worcestershire farms to Birmingham markets.

The north facing Red lion would have been very dark in the 'parlour' and would account for the following less favourable descriptions;

Mr Atack, another Quinton resident who has been an invaluable assistant with research, told me of the days when as a young boy walking from Bearwood to Clent he would stop off with the adults seeking refreshment at The Red Lion. He was not allowed into the pub but would sit in the steep garden at the back facing the fields. He would enjoy his drink and then walk on to Clent not ever crossing a road at all but just walk in green fields all the way. He said, "I have not yet met anyone that remembers The Red Lion as anything other than gloomy dingy place with dark paintwork".

Brett Young once again visits a local establishment for us in *Dr Bradley Remembers* he describes a scene, in North Bromwich, which is known to be Birmingham,

"its landlord a huge, lumbering fellow in the mid forties, with bristling red whiskers and eyebrows and a fiery face and forehead perpetually bedewed with sweat. The little parlour was sunless at the best of times, only dim shapes of tables and chairs and a faint glimmer from the polished brass of the beer engine handles and rows of bottles behind them were visible (pp 125, 210).

There is no indication of this actually being The Red Lion although the description of the parlour fits Mr King's description.

In 1896 a Robert Taylor died at the The Red Lion, he is buried in Quinton cemetery. There is no Mr Taylor on record as ever having worked or owning the pub but my list can hardly be considered a comprehensive one, he could have been a guest who happened to be in there when taken ill, but would it have been so unfortunate to have died glass in hand amidst friends?

In 1931 the relationship between the brewery and the church took a turn for the better as Mitchell's & Butler's donated £10,10s 0d to the Rectory. There are two references to other donations at later dates and although a little late for the reverend Oldfield to have cast judgement one way or another on the offering, I am sure he would have accepted it with good grace and put it to a worthy cause.

When The Red Lion closed its rateable value was placed at £88, a considerable rate, this was because it enjoyed a full on licensee and an off licence. Bass Breweries records reveal that Mitchell's & Butler's purchased the pub off Emma Cheshire on 31st December 1909 for £3000, freehold. The license moved to The Towers on the Walsall Road, it had previously been presumed that as The Red Lion closed and the New Holly Bush opened one day later that the license was transferred locally, however, the records prove this was not the case.

The last landlord to run the Red Lion was Frances E. Bedford; Mitchells & Butler's employed him for the last few months. The pub finally closed its doors on 21st May 1936 and during its last few months, its turnover dropped dramatically as few made the effort to visit the hill.

The last few months barrelage is recorded and reveals its decline;

January - Feb 1936. 97 barrels

March - April 1936. 84 barrels

April - to 21st May 1936. 70 barrels, still a fair consumption considering its size and the local competition, which stood along side the home brewing industry.

The premises were sold to Birmingham Corporation for £1,375; there is no evidence as to how much land was included in Emma Cheshire's sale or the Birmingham Corporations purchase.

Mr Wood occupied one of the cottages on the high bank of land behind the Red Lion prior to the demolition, The family moved from here to further up the Hagley Road to begin Joseph Wood's nurseries, the family ran the three-acre site which reached as far as Harborne until it until the road was widened. Mr Wood was in the Christ Church Quinton Choir and also served as a sidesman. He lived to the ripe old age of 93 and is buried at Quinton.

There are several poems about the pubs in Quinton, one of which is referred to by Rosser and this shorter one recited by Lucy Dearn from c1920-30.

The dog bite the Lion

Drink the Holly Bush dry

Turn the Beech tree inside out

And let the Cock and Magpie fly

<u>Response 2000</u>

The Dog ruled the Lion

The Holly Bush, Carver

Cock and Magpie flown the nest.

Beech tree turned to Amber

The Post office on Quinton Hill next to the Red Lion Public house.

Post office records in the London archive refer to it as

Ridacre, Quinton, Quainton and Queynton.

Other than The Hawthorn Farm plan, there is little to suggest that there was ever another post office sited in the Quinton area other than Alford's. They ran the post office in Quinton for many years and only recently retired after long service, which they had moved from Walters Road to the current position (which is now under threat). There are some photographs of the old site but other than that, there has been very little other information on the post offices in Quinton.

That is until a trip to the Post Office Heritage office in London revealed a little more than had previously been known. The heritage centre its self was not difficult to find but the records within it were. The very large dusty old books are all indexed but many of the actual articles are missing, having been lost during transit for the duration of the war, some by fire and others deemed no longer worthy of keeping. Such a shame, so much is lost to an area when it moves off its home ground or is thrown away. Not all was lost though and there was some new information which came to light. Interestingly enough what did appear was the change and variations on the spelling of Quinton. These variations meant that it was difficult to establish if it was the same place, but fortunately, the article referred to the area and it noted either "on the Birmingham Road to Worcester Road" or some such additional proof.

We take the delivery of post very much for granted today but it is interesting to see how the Royal Mail has evolved. These snippets from the post office archives enable us to view the service from its roots and rediscover what our forebears endured. In order to make sense of some of the entries I have included some of the post office details.

1635   Proclamation of King Charles 1. He allows the public to use "his mail" service.

1677   The franchising is discontinued. The duke of York and Colonel Roger Whitley take over the management of the post office.

1793   London's general "post carriers" receive an official uniform.

1769   Daily postal communications between Birmingham Dudley, Halesowen, Stourbridge, Kidderminster and Bewdley was established.

1832   "John Barrett, a letter carrier is the last post office employee to be hung for stealing mail".

1844   Queynton
"The application for an official post at Queynton is refused. The number of letters from Queynton averages only 20 a week and including all the surrounding villages that can be included in a foot messengers walk falls short of 100 a week, this is too few".

1844   The Ridgacre township plan of 1844 does not indicate where the post office was, but this is probably because of it being a sub post office possibly part of the pub/shop.

1846   January. Book post begins. All books newspapers and other printed paper in open covers can be sent at special lower rate.

1846   "Application for official post. Correspondence of Quainton and surrounding villages Response; considered not sufficient for an official post delivery".

1851   "Reference to Quintain, missing" (When asked for any further information on this missing item, the reply was "there was none to be had". The only thing they could confirm was that it was the correct spelling as recorded and was same place.

1853   The first pillar-boxes are set up on the main land Britain.

1854   Rowland Hill appointed secretary to the Post Office.

1854   Quinton post office.5 miles outside of Birmingham close to Halesowen 2 miles away. Run by J Deeley.

1854   "an allowance of 5/- a week to sub post master at Quinton. For providing a delivery of letters at Bartley Green".

Reference to Quintain (parts missing)"

"Measures sanctioned 28th March 1853 have not been carried out because better measures are proposed. In view of the alterations, sub post master at Quinton to be paid £5.00 per year." (perhaps this is referring to the first move, there were several moves before settling to it current position by the church, the later being from being on the corner of College Road).

1855   Maps shows post office (sub) on the plan of Hawthorn Farm next to the Red Lion Public House. This would suggest that the alteration mentioned in 1854 may have been the move from the hill. The post office then had a second home not far from its existing position before moving over to Walters Road and then back many years later to it current position by the Church.

1881   Mrs Hannah Deeley Postmistress and shopkeeper age 47 widow. From Postal guide. Quinton 5 miles from Birmingham, 2 miles from Halesowen. (She is listed in the census of 1881 as living with daughters Elizabeth Jane, her mother Maria Coley and two sons, William age 12, and James age 9).

1907   Kelly's directory lists Mrs Hannah Deeley as postmistress and provision keeper.

1920   Archive registration 23746. Records of a temporary postman B.S. Price. There appears to have been a problem with the posting of letters as some important documents have been reported as missing, as J Deeley is still post / master/mistress it is she that takes the reprimand. The record notes; "J Deeley has been reprimanded for the loss of regular letters and the irregular treatment of the register!"

Lot 11

**A piece of Land Possessing a very long frontage to two Roads, called Shop Close, containing
1 acre, 2 roots, 8 poles or thereabouts.
This became Trevanie Avenue and the Hagley Road West, the shape has remained largely unchanged,
as can be seen on the plan for the farm.**

HOLLY BUSH HILL, QUINTON.

Figure 87 The Trev-Annie field, Quinton Heights.

Having seen an enlargement of this picture, closer inspection reveals three people under the tree on the right hand side, they all appear to be standing and facing the camera poised and ready. This once arable land had a few cottages that dotted upon the hill, there are references to these cottages and their occupants in the Trevanie Avenue deeds, which the Partridge family were kind enough to allow access.

The Partridge family deeds go back as far as 1876 when Edward Billington died and passed this portion of land to his wife and family. Edward was a gentleman from Warwick, he died on 8th November 1877 after preparing his will a year earlier. Edward left all his possessions to his wife Ann along with a legacy of £100 for her personal use and £19.19 shillings to each of his his trustees, Thompson Forster of Daventry a surgeon and close friend and Colonel John Henry Lowndes, who he instructed to sell all his land and farming implements after his death. There is a reference to Hubert Loxley a publisher in Birmingham selling to the Mucklows' in 1936 but there remains a void from 1877 until that point.

The field (figure 87) is the one highlighted for acquisition for the Mucklow Garage. In 1937, Trevor Mucklow leased the land out in building plots, which was at that time called "Quinton heights estate" at Quinton. He sold the leases for terms of 99 years from 29th September 1936 at the yearly rent of six pounds and ten shillings and the houses sold at £600. The Garage is now the B P garage and Trevor Mucklow and his wife Annie are immortalised in the name "Trev" "Annie" Avenue.

The deeds reveal a few inhabitants to the cottages scattered upon the hill for instance, in 1896, Sarah Elizabeth Edmonds and James Cooper leased the land off Ann Billington and her family, familiar names to the local folk of the area. Then in 1881 Robert Lenton a coachbuilder from 'Mucklow Cottage' at Halesowen moved to Red Lion Hill, Quinton where he rented one of the cottages. Finally in 1937 Doris Evelyn Collet moved from her cottage at 715 Hagley Road West, on the hill into one of the newly built houses on Trevanie Avenue purchasing it for £420 and a yearly lease hold payment of six pounds to Trevor Mucklow.

Public footpath at Quinton.

At Birmingham quarter sessions to be held on April 5th application will be made for

an order for the stopping of two public footpaths at Quinton, one leading from

Hagley Rd West to Ridgacre lane and the other leading from Ridgacre Lane and

connecting with the first Footpath. It is proposed to substitute new highways, one

Clydesdale Rd which is already in existence and the other will be known.

Figure 88 The Smethwick Telephone 6th Feb 1936
demonstrates the exchange of rural footpaths to more efficient roads and pavements.

The footpath which made its way across this field is said to be the same track that led the White Friars across the land. This is mentioned by Rosser who claims that

"additional maps from the last century show a track from the Abbey running north easterly via Howley Grange Farm, crossing Stoney Lane and following the same route as the present walkways. After running the length of what is now Trevanie Avenue it fades out. It likely continued to Warley and the farmland there, which Lady Joan de Botetourt bequeathed to the Abbey in the fourteenth century. (Rosser 1999.189).

Lot 12

A rich and productive meadow.
Called ROUNDABOUT, and surrounded by good roads, containing 2 acres, 1 root,
36 poles or thereabouts.

This final lot of the farm gives us the triangle today of Quinton Lane, Green Lane and Ridgacre lane, It is a pleasant suburb of Quinton without any unwelcome additions; It's traffic although increasing poses a calmer route than the main road can offer.

There we have the final and concluding lot from the sale of 1855, a closing chapter in the history of The Hawthorn Farm, The Hawthorns and part of the rural journey into Birmingham. Directions into Birmingham from Christ Church, The Quinton would once have read, "go down Red Lion Hill into The Hawthorns, go along The Turnpike road, past the Hawthorn Farm on your left, take the road that bends towards the left and go up Holly Bush hill into Beech Lanes and from there …". Neither the road names, nor such a pronounced bend in the road exists any more, these names are lost to us now in our daily lives and recaptured here in part at least (as this is not a full or definitive account) to be acknowledged as part of our local history.

Extract from *The Betrayal*

By the time I had got to where I had no intention of going

Half a lifetime had passed.

I'd sleepwalked so long, while I dozed

Houses outside which gas lamps had spluttered

Were pulled down and replaced,

And my background was wiped from the face of the earth.

****

There was so much I ought to have recorded

So many lives that have vanished-

Families, neighbours, people whose pockets

Were worn thin by hope. They were

The loose change history spent without caring.

Now they have become the air I breathe,

Not to have marked their passing seems such a betrayal.

****

I did not see the grief they were grasping.

The seed of my long alienation from those I loved

Was wrapped in daydreams.

Something I've never been able to pinpoint

Led me away from the blood I ought to have recorded

I search my history for reasons, for omens. But what use now

Zodiacs, or fabulous and complicated charts

Offered up by fly-brained astrologers?

What use now supplications?

****

In the crowd entrails I constantly failed

To read the true nature of my betrayal.

What those who shaped me could not articulate

Still howls for recognition as a century closes,

And their homes are pulled down and replaced,

And their backgrounds are wiped from the face of the earth.

****

by Brian Patten

BIBLIOGRAPHY

Askwith, B. *The Lyttletons' Chatto and Windus*.1975.

Brett Young, Francis. *Dr Bradley Remembers.* The Book Club. 1938.

Brett Young, Francis. *They Seek a Country*. The Book Club. 1937.

Cornwell, Bernard. *History of numbers in regiments from "Eagle".*
     Harper Collins Publishers Ltd; New Ed. 1 April 1994.

Deeley, Catherine. *The Church in the Park.* Messengers. 1956.

Glover, Michael. *The Peninsular War, 1807-1814: A Concise Military History*
     David and Charles (Holdings) Ltd.1974.

Hackwood, F.W. *Oldbury and Round About.* Whitehead Bros. 1915.

Holloway, Roger. *The Queens Own West Kent Regiment.* Leo Coope Ltd.1973.

Hunt,John, Dixon. *The Figure in the Landscape: Poetry, Painting, and Gardening During the Eighteenth Century.* Johns Hopkins University Press, 1976.

Joslin, E C. A. R Litherland. Simpkin, B T. *British Battles and Medals*
     Spink & Son Ltd. London. 1988.

Kelly's Directory, 95th edition .Surrey. October. 1962.

Mackay, J. & Mussell, J .W. (ed*): The Medal Yearbook 2001.* Token Publishing Ltd, Devon.

Madison, John. *Oldbury and Rowley Regis in Old photographs.* Alan Sutton Publishers Ltd.1991.

Maxam, A. *Quinton on Old Picture postcards.* Reflections of a Bygone Age. 1999.

Patten, Brian. *Armada* Flamingo. 1996.

Rosser, Anthony, N. *Quinton and Roundabout Volume one.*The Quinton History Society. 1998.

Rosser, Anthony, N. Quinton and Roundabout Volume two. The Quinton History Society.1999.

Smith, Digby. *The Greenhill Napoleonic war data.* Greenhill Books. 1998.

Stevens, Frank. *The Chapel of Cradley* Mark and Moody. 1933.

Wright, Philip. *Monumental Inscriptions in Jamaica* 1662 -1880. London. 1966.

Electronic resources

Valentine,L. Picturesque England: Its Landmarks and Historical Haunts, As Described in Lay and Legend, Song And story. Hagley Park. http://www.mspong.org/picturesque/hagley_park.html Timbs [Jan.21.2008].

Wellingtons archives http: www.wtj.com/archives/wellington/wells 5 11b.htm Timbs May01.2008].

Painted Illustrations

Fig. 9.   Copenhagen on fire because of British bombardment in 1807, painting by C.W. Eckersberg. Coloured engraving. The Danish Royal Library.

Fig 12.   87th Brian Palmer 87th Regiment at the battle of Vittoria (76cm x 51cm), oil on canvas. Scotland. Cranston Fine Art. Scotland. www. directcart.co.uk.Cranston Fine Art). [08.05.2008.

Fig 6.   Chris, Collingwood. *Advance on Vittoria Oil* on canvas (64cm x 38cm. Cranston Fine Art. Scotland. www. directcart.co.uk.Cranston Fine Art). [08.05.2008.

Other Sources.

Birmingham archives:
> Abstract of marriage settlement of Colonel Charles Hill and AnnTroughton. MS3101/A/B/7/13 *1855*.
> The Hawthorn Farm details Sc47.
> Troughton wills MS927/67.
> Galton file, Norton 2837.
> Lyttelton's file Ms 9271-1.

Birmingham Council.

Birmingham Library.

Brandhall Library.

Codsall Library.

Dudley Library.

Fiftieth Regiment of Foot, The Queens own Regiment. Archives.

Hereford and Worcester record Office.AK 53.

Mitchell's and Butler's archives.

National post office archives.

Pie's directory.

Private family papers.

Private papers from the Browning family.

Private papers belonging to The Hassell family.

Private family papers belonging to The Parton family.

Private family papers belonging to the Witcomb family.

Quinton Oracle. Issue Number 4, The Millennium edition.

Quinborne Library.

Shropshire records and research.
> The sale documents of Hawthorn Farm, Ref 4752/6/33,4752.3/8.

Sketchleys directory.

Swinneys directory.

The Midland advertiser and Wednesbury Borough News.

The Quinton Parish magazine.

The Smethwick Telephone.

The Weekly news.

Worcester Library, for papers and photographs belonging to the Gregory family.

Worcester record AK 53.

Worcester Library for papers and photographs belonging to the Gannon family.

Worcester Library for papers and photographs belonging to the Powell family.

Worcester Library for papers and photographs belonging to the Saunders family.

Index